T0194625

God Thoughts 2 U

Has the church been misinformed and sabotaged?

K Edward (Ed) Balentine

WESTBOW
PRESS®
A DIVISION OF THOMAS NELSON
& ZONDERVAN

Scripture quotations marked KJV taken from the
King James Version of the Bible.

Scripture quotations marked AMP are taken from the Amplified Bible,
Copyright © 2015 by The Lockman Foundation. Used by permission.

WestBow Press books may be ordered through booksellers or by contacting:

WestBow Press
A Division of Thomas Nelson & Zondervan
1663 Liberty Drive
Bloomington, IN 47403
www.westbowpress.com
1 (866) 928-1240

ISBN: 978-1-9736-6206-8 (sc)
ISBN: 978-1-9736-6208-2 (hc)
ISBN: 978-1-9736-6207-5 (e)

Library of Congress Control Number: 2019906878

Print information available on the last page.

WestBow Press rev. date: 06/06/2019

Contents

Endorsements

Ed Balentine writes words of Life from his personal relationship with God. He has a unique ability to express great truth and insight with clarity, humility, and compassion. – Becki L., Virginia

Ed Balentine has some keen insights, interesting perspectives, and unusual angles on the intersection of the Kingdom of God with everyday life, and expresses them in a unique voice. Fun and enlightening reading! Chuck B., Pennsylvania

I've known Ed for forty-five years and have always found his ministry to be edifying and insightful and that he has a gift for making deeper truths understandable, well balanced and down-to-earth - something anyone can understand and grow from hearing. It is a pleasure to participate to this small degree in seeing his work published, for he has a gift for expressing God's Truth in ways that bypass many folks' instinctive recoil from Christianity. Eds' writing style is personal and unique in my experience, and many of the things he writes provoke me to write my own understanding of things I believe are profitable for the committed Christian desiring fruitful fellowship with Christ. His writing inspires serious contemplation in me that few manage to stimulate. Much of what he writes bears the evidence of having been purchased through suffering, hardships, mistakes and sorrows, but it is clear in reading his material that he has held on and steadfastly turned to the Lord in the forty-five years I known him as both minister and personal friend. Jon T., Florida

Introduction

A few people have asked questions about stuff I have written, so I thought I would try to give some answers . . . here we go:

One sister asked me, regarding a short thing I had written, whom I was quoting. I answered something along the lines that I wasn't quoting anyone that I knew. On further reflection, it is clear to me that I have gleaned from MANY teachers and writers over the years, and have without doubt absorbed truth from many. I owe a debt to these men and women, and I am thankful. However, if I am AWARE that I am quoting someone, I aim to make certain that that person is credited: otherwise, I am writing what I think I am hearing from the Lord, recognizing all the while that although I am "hearing" it now, it was more than likely "spoken" some time ago by someone else: most certainly if it was God then who knows "when" He spoke it?

A brother asked what prompted me to write this or that . . . the simplest, and truest answer is that I believe God prompted me to write, and best I could, I aimed to convey in writing that which I believed He was prompting. I am not at all certain of any other thing that I could say "prompted me" to write . . . however, see the below:

One area of my life where I think I see the Lord wanting to transform me is where I had felt I needed to know the end of a thing before I was willing to start it . . . a paraphrase of a quote (somewhere) is that if a person wanted to be led by the Spirit of God, he/she must abandon all thoughts of "outcome" . . . like Joshua, being told to have everyone march around Jericho in silence for six days, and then on the seventh . . . you know . . . or Gideon being told, among other things to whittle his "army" down to 300 men, then to "arm" them with pitchers and candles . . . etc. . . and we all know that story. I'm not trying to compare myself with those or with other men, but they help me understand why not knowing how a thing is going to turn out should not prevent me from doing the thing I believe I have heard Him say to me. So, for the most part, I do not know why He gives me this or that to write, or who His intended "target" is.

Presently, I am hoping for some feedback, since I am very aware that as early brother Paul wrote, we see through a glass, dimly: We know in PART; that some plant, others water but only God gives the increase. Of course SOME just blow off steam, which Paul used other words to say.

Since the late 1960s I have been asking the Lord to show me Himself, and to learn His ways. I think He has been doing that since then (and probably before then). Part of that has been an increasing awareness of the chasm between what is currently "seen", by that which calls itself the church, of the Lord and His ways . . . the chasm (and I think it is a WIDE chasm) between that "perception" (deception??) and the truth . . . so I THINK this has something to do with why I write what I write.

I have also become acutely aware in the process of trying to write about something that there is MUCH more that could truthfully be said about that subject. That is in part why I hope for some response from those who read. I am thankful for those who HAVE responded, and hope for more.

Then there is the inherent problem with communication

in general: I think most of us are too aware of the potential problems that exist, trying to convey ANYTHING. We try to say something as well as we can, and sometimes we do that quite well, and sometimes we don't, but then is the question of whether or not the thing that our audience "hears" is the same thing we thought we were saying . . .

Then of course there is always the question which I believe I have sensed (though of course perhaps not, since no one has actually SAID it) of "who are YOU to write such stuff?" . . . to which I can only respond that I am "me": one of God's creations, bent in my own peculiar ways, whom God may have chosen from a crowded field of others of His creation bent in THEIR own peculiar ways, to write such stuff for the benefit (hopefully) of some of those others, as yet undisclosed to me.

Graham Cooke once said that he thought his ministry was to present Christ to the church . . . I resonate with that idea. I think that we (myself included) have been seduced away from the simplicity, the truths, and the power of His Life in us, and I would like to be one voice among (hopefully) many who will call us back to that which is truly of Him.

Jesus said that the Words He spoke were spirit, and they were truth . . . though of course MANY did not see, hear, or understand Him; nonetheless it is a goal of mine to also speak that which is spirit and truth . . . God help me . . . that those whom He has prepared may hear and be built up in Him.

So I do not have an "intended audience", though I THINK it would primarily be "the church". I have two hopes regarding these writings: First, that some who read will offer response, to fill out, correct, or whatever might be helpful, that which I have written in order that next, something might be presented to the church for our building and growth and strengthening.

Creation Equation

*"the Lord God formed man from the dust of the ground,
and breathed into his nostrils the breath of Life, and
man became a Living soul"* Genesis 2:7, KJV.

. . . the record of our beginnings . . .

There have been quite a few teachings going around about how we are made: most say that we are body, soul, and spirit; that our body is the physical "part" of us, our soul is an invisible "part" which is made up of our intellect, our emotions, and our will; and our spirit is also an invisible "part" in which our conscience and intuition dwell which, most say, represents the "real us".

Ought we not pay more attention to the scriptural account of our beginnings? We are told that He FORMED us from the dust of the earth; sounds quite like that would be our body: nothing but a shell, with nothing living in it. But then He breathed into us His breath, and we BECAME a LIVING SOUL . . . so all of those invisible qualities came into existence WHEN HE BREATHED INTO US THE BREATH OF LIFE.

SO . . . we <u>BECAME</u> a living soul . . . not "we were GIVEN" a soul . . . we <u>BECAME</u> a living soul, so, if we <u>BECAME</u> something, we must <u>BE</u> that something: a soul. We <u>ARE</u> a soul, and the makeup of that soul is a lifeless body, into which has been breathed our spirit; our spirit, which is designed to give us the ability to interact with both what we call the "Natural" world. (the natural world in which we live) AND the supernatural world. (the Kingdom of God) We were designed to LIVE in BOTH realms, at all times: the five physical senses by which we interact with the natural world, and the two "spiritual" senses (conscience and intuition) by which we interact with the spiritual, invisible world (Kingdom of God).

So, the soul which we ARE . . . where IS it, and what is its function? What does it (what do WE) DO? That "us" (the soul) is the "us" who receives input all the time from both the outside world and the spirit realm . . . that "us" continuously perceives things from both realms, and evaluates them both (our intellect), determining what effect, if any, they have on US (our emotions), and makes decisions about what, if anything, we will DO (our will).

Scripture says that the SOUL that sins will die: so what dies? our body or our spirit ? In the beginning we were made to be perfect: all of our "parts" functioned absolutely according to design, our five physical senses and our two spiritual senses were fully alive and functioning absolutely as they were created to function . . . but then Adam and Eve . . .

Adam and Eve: how long did they live that perfect life, fully alive and functioning? For some time (a day? . . . a week ? . . . a month? . . a year? . . . many years? . . . decades? . . . or maybe longer) . . . we don't know . . . but at some point the tempter entered the picture. He entered that perfect existence in that perfect garden, and assaulted them; wore them down; persuaded them that God was holding something back from them; that God didn't mean what He said when He warned them that if they ate from the fruit of that tree of the knowledge of good and evil, they would surely die. The tempter told them they would NOT surely die, but rather would become like God, knowing good and evil for themselves . . . well, God later said that they HAD become like one of them, knowing good and evil, and because of that, they were barred from the garden. They were then dead . . . not yet in their physical bodies . . . their soul died . . . the "them" of them died . . . why? because in taking it upon themselves to know for themselves what was good and evil, they had rejected the Life they had received at their creation, thinking they could manage their lives better separate from the One who had created them. They would do it themselves, they thought, but they did not have it within themselves to make their lives better . . . or even good . . . they had pushed out LIFE . . . they died.

Think about when you cut a daisy out of your garden to put in a vase in your kitchen: the moment you cut the stem of that daisy, it DIES. You have severed it from its connection to life, and it is dead. It doesn't LOOK dead for some time, especially if you put it in water, and it will LOOK alive for some time, but from the moment you cut its stem, it was dead . . . and so it was for Adam and Eve . . . they LOOKED alive for a long time, but they were actually dead from the moment they pushed God, AS GOD (Who is the only life there is) out of their lives.

So . . . at that point we (humans) came into the world . . . with a body, and also with a spirit . . . almost as at the beginning . . . almost, but not quite. We had a spirit, but Life was not in it . . . We had banished Life from our beings by substituting our own selves for Life. We did not know that: the tempter did not tell us that part . . . neither did he tell us that apart from Life, we would not have any capacity to order our lives according to our Maker's intentions.

No longer would our two spiritual senses (our conscience

and intuition) serve us truly. The power for them to operate as they were designed was no longer there. Life was gone, and they could only function superficially . . . and not only that, but that same Life no longer was there to enable the five physical senses to be reliable for us. It was Life (GOD) Who caused all the senses to function properly, and without Him (Life), NOTHING works right.

We ("our soul") does not have the correct input coming through our five physical senses and our two spiritual ones: WE ("our soul"), because we no longer have reliable input, CANNOT truly understand things . . . cannot accurately "feel" things, and therefore cannot make adequate use of our wills. Our choices are skewed, because our avenues of input are stunted . . . warped . . mangled . . . at very best, incomplete. Yes, "we" still have "us" . . . "I" still have "me" . . . still "have", yet more truly AM a soul . . . BUT it is a DEAD soul. We pushed Life out, so now we are left with death.

BUT . . . JESUS . . . in the fullness of time, Jesus . . . And now we have another option! He came to give Life: that which we had lost. To any of us who would "Believe on HIM" . . . To any of us who will believe in; trust in; rely on ; "bet our bottom dollar", so to speak, ON HIM, not depending to any degree on any other thing . . . To those of us who will do that, we will be given back that Life which we lost. We will again BECOME a LIVING soul; WE will be ALIVE . . . FOREVER !!!!!!!

So . . . now . . . LIFE has entered our being and made a new creation: a new, ALIVE "soul" . . . A new "us", WITH LIFE AT ITS CENTER. And now our senses: our seeing, hearing, touching, tasting, and smelling as well as our conscience and intuition are infused with LIFE. They can function as they are intended to function, which can cause our soul; our "us" to rightly exercise our intellect; our emotions; and our will . . .

the "us" which is a new creature . . . Christ in us, the hope of glory . . . rescued from death and placed into LIFE. He, once again, has breathed into our bodies, and we again have BECOME (not "been given") a LIVING SOUL.

a "Y"

OK . . . so I'm driving along down a road, and ahead of me I see that the road splits left and right: a "Y" . . . the sign over the left split reads "To Life", and the sign over the right split reads "Easier: More Fun". Well, ONE thing I know is that if I want to continue driving ahead, I gotta decide which of these I'm gonna take, but the problem is that I've never gone on either of those roads before, so how am I gonna be able to decide? So I pull off just before the "Y", and get out to walk a mile or so down each road to get some idea of what I'm deciding. The road to the left, with the "To Life" sign turns into a gravel road quite quickly, and as I walk along, I see that it has a lot of sharp turns in it . . . and it gets pretty narrow . . . and there are a bunch of potholes and bumps (some big stones). I can tell this will not be an easy road to take, but the plus side is that it <u>IS</u> supposed to lead "to life" . . . I'll check out the "Easier, more fun" one, I think, so back I go, and start down THAT road: it's VERY wide . . . and it is quite straight, with only a few gentle curves in it . . . and it's smooth . . can't see a bump anywhere . . . a very nice-looking road, to be sure, and it has been landscaped, with lots of shrubs and flowers on either side. This would certainly be a pleasant road to go on, and I could definitely get there much faster than I could on that other road, but it does not say "To Life", and I AM really interested in Life . . . so . . . what to do??? I think I'll just sit here in my car for a while and take some time to make my decision, but after an hour or so a cop car comes up beside me, and the cop tells me I can't just sit there, even if I AM off the side and not in any travel lane. I have to move SOMEWHERE, he says, so OK, I gotta move . . . but WHERE? I see three options: drive ahead to the left, "To Life"; drive ahead to the right, "Easier, More Fun"; or turn around and go back where I came from. The fourth option of just sitting there in my car is not an option any more: they won't let me do it . . . so . . . I may not just sit here, but even if I could, it would not be going "To Life", Neither would going back take me "To Life", and neither would taking the "Easier, More Fun" road take me "To Life" . . . looks like if I want to go "To Life", I'll HAVE to drive on THAT road . . . but it's so rough, and narrow, and bumpy, and SO not straight . . . so crooked . . . can hardly see any distance in front of me . . . How do I even know if the sign is true? What should I do?

Are You Saved?

Are you saved? is a question I used to hear asked quite a bit in my earlier years (yes, I <u>DID</u> have some earlier years) . . . the "recommended" answer I used to hear was "yes, I *have been* saved; I *am being* saved; and I *shall be* saved". I suppose in a way that sorta "nutshells" it: you know, there was a date and time when I "asked Jesus into my heart", or some other similar phrase; a point in time when I first believed: then comes all my days between that day and the day when I go to see Jesus (the process that goes on throughout my life (which the theologians call "sanctification"); and, at last, the day when I am <u>FINALLY</u> "saved" ("in heaven")

I have a notion that God doesn't see it quite the same, since He is not bound by time as we are and so He does not necessarily need a rigid sequence of events such as WE are prone to accept, though it does sorta help us understand the basics. There <u>WAS</u> a time I believed the gospel; my life goes on for however long, during which as He is able, He transforms me into His image; and of course there <u>WILL</u> come a time when this earthly life ends, and I move on to a realm where all kinds of sin and its' effects will no longer exist . . . I think we will take a closer look at the middle (sanctification) part at some future time, but for this writing I thought to ask the question "from what am I saved"?

So . . . from what <u>AM</u> I saved? Well one scripture tells us we are saved from darkness to light; from death to life . . . and the most typical answer I have heard is that He saves us FROM SIN . . . but what does THAT mean? That we are saved from committing murder? From lying? from committing adultery? from coveting? I think from these and many more things which ARE, of course, sins, and if ya wanna include things like what we read in I Corinthians 13, Matthew 5, 6, & 7, Luke 6, and the many instructions scattered throughout the scriptures about how life oughtta be lived, THEN a huge list develops of sins . . . and we, in the eternal sense, are saved from them all, and since nothing of sin can enter "heaven", all THAT will then be gone, and we will then have been totally *"saved"* . . . from sin . . . so if we look at our 3-step approach, it certainly looks like we are in that second stage . . . sanctification . . . *"being saved"* . . . but really, what IS this sin from which we are *"being saved"* and from which we SHALL BE saved ?

MY thought is that all that goes back to the Garden of Eden, when our great-greats decided to make their OWN choices for and by themselves, denying God His rightful place of authority and control: they ate some of *the fruit of the tree of the knowledge of good and evil* . . . they became their own gods; decided their OWN decisions according to THEIR limited knowledge . . . but what happened *which they did NOT know* is that by doing that they barred entry of the ONLY LIFE which exists . . . barred it from their own beings: no Life allowed . . . and so death was the inevitable option. It was, and still is, a true issue of Life . . . and death.

So OK, we are saved from death . . . certainly . . . BUT all of us have been raised eating from the tree of the knowledge of good and evil: we have not known another way . . . and it is THIS death . . . THIS SIN . . . from which we have been and are being and will be saved.

So we have been saved by believing Gods' provision for us: Jesus dying on that cross, taking on Himself the death penalty which was ours because we have been eating from that same tree . . . He has removed that death from us, but that is not all: not only has He removed that death from us, He has given us HIS LIFE . . . and it is HIS LIFE IN US which makes our "sanctification" (our "being saved") not only a possibility, but a fact: we ARE "being saved"

So lest we skip by and therefore do not know or understand what it is from which were, are, and shall be saved, let me ask this question: WHO IS IT who decides (in each of our lives) to eat from (and try to live by) the fruit of the tree of the knowledge of good and evil . . . TODAY ? . . . I am thinking it is US OURSELVES . . . which means (how much time do you spend trying to figure out whether this thing or that thing is "good" or "bad" ? How frequently do we judge ourselves or other people by that standard?) . . . and so it means . . . it means that it is, in truth, US . . OUR . . SELF . . . from which we are being saved !

He is saving us by progressively delivering us from the effects of us "eating from OUR tree of the knowledge of good and evil" . . . helping us to abandon THAT way of trying to "live" by leading and bringing us to where we will live from that OTHER tree: the Tree of Life, which IS HIMSELF . . . SAVED!

Absolutes ???

Is there such a thing as absolute truth? Absolute Right? Absolute Wrong? If not, then who is to say whatever anyone does is either right or wrong?

Beheading Christians and children and others? Those who are doing it think it's right . . . Cutting someone off in traffic? THEY think it's OK . . . Breaking into someone's house & stealing their stuff? OK by them . . . Doing Drugs? Selling Drugs? Killing babies before they're born? Killing an adult? Lying? Cheating on income taxes? Having sex with someone not yours? Having same-sex sex? Divorcing your mate? Cheating on an exam? Dishonoring your parents? Not forgiving someone? Gossiping?

Who is to decide these things? Oh, I know . . . it's YOU . . . YOU decide about all this stuff, plus a lot more . . . you've already decided about some of the things I've just written, haven't you? so fill in the blank with YOUR name: _____ decides! Right?

Or maybe you think everybody should decide for themselves what's right or wrong? . . . that works pretty well . . . well, at least until one of them decides to do one of those things to YOU (or someone you love) . . . I'm thinking THEN you might change your mind about letting everyone decide for themselves??? . . so now we're back to YOU again, I think . . . but then, I don't like THAT very much because I think it should be ME who gets to decide. That would be OK, right? No?

Oh my, it looks to me like we're in some sort of mess here . . . unless . . . UNLESS there actually IS absolute truth somewhere? Absolute right? Absolute wrong? But if there actually IS absolute (anything), how can I find it? Some folks say, "just read yer Bible" . . . but I know there are hundreds (if not thousands, maybe millions) of different groups, all claiming to base their beliefs on the Bible, who can't seem to agree on what the Bible really says . . . and many of the more "enlightened" folk say ya gotta be careful about that book . . . parts of it are 6,000 years old, for Pete's sake . . . surely we are a much better educated and enlightened society than THAT ?

So now it's back to YOU . . . (or ME) . . .

But what if there is a BEING who is actually Knowledgeable & wise enough to decide everything? What if there IS such an One? . . . and what if THAT One is also unlimited in authority and power? . . . What then?

And while I'm on this, what about enlightenment? What if we've been lied to about enlightenment? What if it isn't enlightenment after all? What if it's actually darkening? What then?

Decisions, Decisions

Decisions, decisions, decisions! seems like there's no way to avoid 'em . . . all the time . . . no end to 'em ! Decision after decision after decision, so it seems: and actually so it IS, cuz life goes on moment after moment, and MOST of those moments require that some sort of decision must be made, and WE hafta make 'em! They don't give us no choice!

So many situations with so many decisions . . . we get hungry, so we decide to eat (or if we have decided ahead of time to fast from food for a while, then we decide NOT to eat even if we ARE hungry); we get sleepy so we decide to get some sleep (unless our boss tells us we need to work three or four more hours: THEN we decide to postpone our sleep for three or four hours). We might be tempted to think our boss MADE us postpone our sleep, but still it was US who decided to do it, most likely because we decided it was more important to keep our job than it was to get to sleep three or four hours earlier; or someone does us wrong and we decide to sue them in court, or we decide to forgive 'em, or someone sues US in court and we decide to defend ourselves and fight back and get our rights, or we decide NOT to resist in court. We decide to be sexually pure, or we decide to "have an affair" or we decide to become promiscuous; we decide to pay the IRS ALL our taxes due, or we decide to cheat on our taxes. And these are only a

FEW of the many decisions we hafta make in the course of our moments.

Somewhere I read that we make an average of 35,000 decisions every day of our lives . . . wow, really? . . . of course most of 'em are "sub-conscious", like the decisions to make very minor corrections on our steering wheel as we drive along, in response to differing road conditions . . . did you ever try not moving your steering wheel when you're driving? Try it sometime (but just for a very short time . . . it's usually best to stay on the road)

So somebody offers us a gift . . . we are free to decide to take it or not to take it, our decision: we have to make SOME decision. We could, of course, decide not to decide right then, which means that at least for NOW we have decided NOT to take it, though it might be possible to take it later . . . but for NOW we have decided NOT to take it, which means (at least for now) that we will NOT receive the benefit of that gift, whatever that might be. If we want to get the benefit of the gift, we MUST decide to reach out our hand and take it.

God, for example, has offered us many gifts, together with instructions about how we may receive them. The most important gift He has offered us is an unending Life, and He told us how we may reach out and take it. We are yet always free to take it or to refuse it or to wait, but if we decide to wait we have by default chosen NOT to take it right now.

So in all the moments of our lives and at all our decision points, whatever decisions we make have some sort of consequence, about which we have NO choice. If I choose NOT to accept some gift, I will absolutely NOT get the benefit of that gift, and I will live, at least until I decide otherwise, a life without that benefit. We may choose anything we want at our many decision points: in fact we MUST choose SOMETHING at all of those points and every choice leads to an effect about which we have no choice. I'm thinking many of us would like to make decisions and NOT have consequences, but it don't work that way. Even NOT deciding on a thing is in itself a choice, with its attending effect.

Decisions, Decisions, Decisions

the Two Trees

I'm thinking everybody has heard about how God made a man (the very first one ever), and plunked him down in a fantastic garden. He (the man) lived there quite a while by himself (except of course for a bunch of animals which God had also made). God came by and chatted with him pretty regularly, and for a while everything was great! But after a while God began to notice that he (the man) seemed kinda sad . . . so He (God) asked him (the man) if there was some sort of problem . . . the man said that he really didn't know for sure, but that he had been noticing that the other creatures around him all seemed to have somebody that was like them, "but", the man said, "there isn't anybody like me anywhere in the garden, and somehow this don't feel good to me . . . but I don't know what to do about it" . . . well, God thought about that for a while, and then He (God) said, "ya know, I think you're right: it ain't good . . . but I DO know what to do about it!"

So He (God) put him (the man) into a deep sleep (I don't know how He DONE that, but He IS God, after all), and when he woke up . . . shazam ! . . . right there beside him was this gorgeous creature: a lot like him, but NOT like him in quite a few ways. He (the man) asked Him (God) where that beautiful one came from, and He (God) told him (the man) that while he (the man) was snoozing, He (God) had taken this one OUT OF him (the man). Since the man knew that he WAS a man, and since God had told him that this new creature was taken from inside him, he declared that she must be a woman ("wo"- meaning out of, and man meaning . . . well, you know) so as we have all heard, he (the man) was given the name "Adam" (which means "man of red earth" . . . and since one of the first tasks God had given Adam was to name stuff, he also named the new creature "Eve", which means "revealed", or "to live and breathe" . . . and so it came about that Adam and Eve lived together in the garden . . . It came to be known as "Eden". They say it was in Iraq, somewhere near the Tigris and Euphrates rivers: maybe you could find it if you tried real' hard (though I really doubt it, for reasons I'll talk about later.)

So there they were . . . the man, Adam and his wife, Eve (well, they didn't call her "wife" at that time . . . that was added later . . . another thing to think about, but not for me to write about in this writing). God told them they would be getting hungry every now and then, and when they did, they could eat any of the plants in the garden (or outside it) that made their own seeds (that garden had a bunch of 'em) . . . "AND", God continued, "you may ALSO eat the delicious fruit of all the trees here in the garden (*have you ever had a fresh, tree-ripened peach?*) . . . All, that is, EXCEPT for THAT tree right beside the middle tree. The middle tree is the best of ALL the trees: Eat from it regularly, because when you do, you will live forever! It is the Tree of Life ! . . . BUT . . . that other tree right beside it is toxic. Avoid it at ALL COSTS ! It is the Tree of the Knowledge of Good and Evil, and its fruit is always fatal for any man or woman who eats it . . . the moment you eat it is the moment you will die. Do NOT eat the fruit from THAT tree, even if it looks really beautiful !"

Well, after a while a low-down snake slithered up to Eve (it was the very wiliest of God's creatures) and began to talk to her . . . he claimed that when God told her not to eat that fruit, He was keeping something from her . . . that dirty rotten low-down snake told her that she really SHOULD eat some, because it would make her wise, and she would be like God, knowing good and evil, then he told her she could make her OWN decisions. She wouldn't need to only do whatever God said: she could listen to God, of course, but after she had a bite of that fruit, she could decide for herself whether or not to do whatever God was telling her . . . on her own . . .

Well, after a bit she began believing that low-down snake . . . and then she picked one (it really DID look beautiful), and took a bite . . . then she gave a bite to her husband, and HE ate it . . . IMMEDIATELY things changed: a strange sort of darkness came; they became aware that they were naked (they had always been naked, but now they were ashamed); then when they knew that God was coming to spend some time with them (like He always did) suddenly they were afraid . . . AFRAID ? . . . of GOD ? . . . where did THAT come from? And the shame? . . . was this the dying thing God told 'em about?

God told them that yes, this was the beginning of what they would experience, now that they were dead, and things would get much worse as time went on . . . and they DID . . . and it's STILL getting worse and worse today.

Not only that, but that fruit is terribly addicting . . . they had to have more and more of it, all throughout their natural physical lives, and it continues to be addictive to every man, woman, and child for thousands of years, right up to and including today.

So now, Adam and Eve had an EXTERNAL "life" . . . that is, ya couldn't tell from looking at them that they were dead inside (they LOOKED alive). It took several hundred years for their bodies to die, but of course eventually their bodies died too . . . ya see, the REAL Adam and Eve (you and me too) is the INSIDE one: what made them THEM (and what makes us US) is the invisible part. We call that our spirit. NOT visible, BUT the real us . . . our body is the place where we live.

When Adam and Eve ate the fruit of that tree (it was not just ANY tree, ya know, or just ANY fruit: it was THE fruit THAT tree produced, knowing good and evil). I think it is worth saying that this "knowing" thing is NOT the sort of thing we think of, like we "know" our A_B_Cs, or we "know" that 2 + 2 = 4 . . . no . . . THIS kind of "Knowing" is more like something penetrates and/or permeates our being, so that it becomes a real part of us. Think about this: they had ALWAYS known good, right? So what got added to their being ? It was EVIL, right? And if we think about it, it was the entrance of evil into their beings that produced their death (and ours too, whenever we eat that fruit). What happens at this point is that God (who IS the ONLY LIFE that exists) was/is expelled. Humans are not designed or equipped to handle that kind of "knowledge" (evil), God (Life) expelled, necessarily leaving death in their/ our spirit.

God USED to be IN them, taking care of everything, but from then on, until Jesus came and died in our place and GAVE us THE ONE AND ONLY LIFE, until that time, God became separated from us humans. LIFE was separated from us, so we have/had a dead spirit which could sustain our physical bodies for a few years . . . not forever . . . ONLY TRUE Life (God) will last forever !

Well (back to the garden) God knew it would be an unspeakable horror for Adam and Eve to live forever in that condition, so He kicked them out of the Garden, and just to be sure they wouldn't sneak back in to get some fruit from the Tree of Life, He stationed an angel there with a fiery sword to keep everybody away. Nobody has ever been able to get to it, though many have looked for it. The Tree of Life is still alive today: not gone, but hidden. Since Jesus, it is still "there" waiting for us, and there is no angel guarding it with a fiery sword . . . its access is totally available today, though the way to it IS narrow . . . to ANYONE who will turn away from the fruit of the tree of the Knowledge of Good and evil, and believe (count on and depend on the work of Jesus on the cross and nothing else).

The tree of the Knowledge of Good and Evil, however, has grown . . . and spread all over the globe . . . it has become SO commonplace; so "usual" that we today don't even recognize it (*do YOU know what it looks like?*) or give it much thought . . . we chow down on its fruit without thinking or knowing what we're doing . . . ALL of us ! We think it's normal . . . We actually delight in it ! . . BUT . . . it is STILL death to us . . . it STILL expels LIFE . . . STILL injects death into our spirits.

Think about it (yes, YOU, Darlin') . . . on what basis do YOU decide stuff (yeah, I know, me too) today? I'm thinkin' that ya mostly decide stuff based on what you think is good (or maybe you DON'T think it's good, but you wanna do it anyway), or ya just FEEL like doing it; maybe you have carefully weighed all the pros and cons; you have considered all the options you can think of before you decided; or maybe you decide to do it based on something somebody told you; or they asked you for something and you decided to give it to them; or you decided NOT to give it to them. Maybe you even thought GOD wanted something from you: so many possibilities! (I'm sure there are many more)

I know that these sorts of ways are how you do it (decide stuff), cuz that's how ALL humans do, ever since the garden of Eden, with the tree of Life, was hidden. It is how we have ALL been taught and trained ever since that day and every day since.

So what? you may be asking . . . well, kids, we got a problem . . . the way we decide stuff IS the problem . . . a serious problem . . . a deadly problem (that all of us have).

Ya see, when Adam and his wife ate the fruit of that tree, they swallowed "the knowledge of good and evil", and along with the actual "knowledge" came the reality that that "knowledge" would be the guiding factor in their lives. God was no longer the source of their "lives". They had effectively kicked God OUT, and since God is the ONLY Life there is, what was left for them (and all of us since) is "no life" . . . (death) . . . it became the guiding force for Adam and Eve and for all their descendants, including you . . . and me. . . God WAS INSIDE His creation . . . but now was outside of it, as it continued to be until Jesus came and died our death.

Now of course throughout history there have been men and women who have heard God telling them to do this or that, or to speak this or that, and who were obedient, so that they brought God's Life into their circumstances in those instances . . . and of course that still happens with some today.

Yet the problem of the death involved is still affecting our "lives" today. ALL of us!: Even those of us who occasionally hear and obey God's direction. We are, in truth, all dead, and that fact means that all our deciding and the stuff we do as a result of that deciding . . . is death . . . and causes further death, wherever it touches! Rather than being "spreaders of Life" (as God intends), we have become destroyers . . . even when we thought what we were doing was GOOD!

Now I know that this is a hard (almost impossible) pill to swallow (for me too) . . . BUT . . . there IS fantastically good news! and the more fully we know and understand our PROBLEM, the more fantastically GOOD this news IS (to us). As an example, when I was diagnosed with cancer, I submitted myself to the advised treatment and now I am cancer-free (good news) . . . BUT . . . if I had been unwilling to accept the fact that I had a cancer, I would most likely not be alive today. It is SO essential to see and accept our problem in order for us to participate in the Good News !

So now, the GOOD news ! . . . around 2,000 years ago, Jesus came from heaven to our earth . . . HE CAME <u>FOR THE SPECIFIC PURPOSE</u> of taking care of our problem, and giving us His Life (the ONLY Life there is, remember?) So He lived here about 33 years, after which He allowed Himself to be horribly beaten, and then killed.

It was God's plan to rescue US. Well, not only did Jesus die, but He took on Himself ALL of OUR deaths (the death we were experiencing, though we didn't know it): the result of doing our own thing. He took it all into Himself! He is God, as well as man, so He could do that . . . so OUR spiritual death (we had dead spirits, remember?) . . . our spiritual death was conquered and undone because He took us INTO Himself, dying in place of us and instead of us! NO MORE SPIRITUAL DEATH FOR US! (us who believe . . . more on that later). So He carried all our self-directed thoughts and words and stuff we did <u>WITH</u> Him (all the death stuff that was us: that was part of us) . . . carried all that with Him when He died . . . took it somewhere we don't know much about for about 3 days, and then His Father, by the power of Holy Spirit, raised Him back to Life! When He died, He took all of us with Him: All that death, on Him . . . BUT . . . when He was brought back to Life, WOW! then there was no death in Him, which means (since we were with Him through the whole thing) that WE did not have any death in US either! We were no longer dead, but ALIVE ! Is that good news, or what? We were ALIVE, with HIS Life ! (the only Life there IS, remember?)

OK . . . so . . . the Bible says it this way (<u>my paraphrase of Romans 5:17 & 18</u>) "Adam's one sin (the one we've been talking about . . . eating from the tree of the knowledge of good and evil) brings condemnation (death) for everyone . . . BUT . . . Christ's one act of righteousness (dying for us) brings a right relationship with God and new life for everyone."

A RECAP

1. - Jesus absorbed our death when He died for us.
2. - He abolished the barrier that our sin had erected between us and God. (so we have free and open access to God)
3. - He showed (in His resurrection) that death has no power over us today.
4. - Not only are our sins forgiven, but WE are forgiven for choosing stuff for and by ourselves.
5. - AND . . . we now have Life . . . HIS Life . . . living inside our bodies!

Well we STILL can (and we still do) "live" (we think) out of the tree of the knowledge of good and evil, The difference is that NOW, because of Jesus, our death has been taken and we have been (and so we ARE) forgiven . . . AND . . . we have real Life !

Because of THAT Life (now inside us), we have the wonderful option of ordering our lives according to THE LIFE of the One Who now lives inside us ! . . . REALLY LIVING !

So the tree of the knowledge of good and evil still exists today, and we grew up and were trained to gobble its fruit. It still cannot produce Life (because it only <u>IS</u> death, of course), but what about the Tree of Life? What happened to it? Is it still hidden? and how do we eat from IT?

I'm thinking that by now you know a little bit about that tree . . . it's the Lord Himself, isn't it? . . . and where is it now, and how do we eat from it ? I bet you know that too, doncha ? it is right inside us, where Jesus "put" it, and we eat of it by a thing called "believing"! First, we believe that we have a problem (as you know, our problem is that we're dead . . . SIN . . . then we believe that Jesus' death and resurrection took care of that sin, and then as that Life within us grows, we continue believing, all through our lives, whatever that Life "says" to us. That's how we get to increasingly Live from that tree of Life, and "live" less and less from that other tree.

Of course this "believing" thing is NOT a mental exercise . . . it is a LIFE . . . it starts with a "Word" spoken in our heart (where Jesus Lives), received by us, similar to the soil in my big pot "receiving" my grapefruit seed that I planted in it (the soil did not plant that seed in itself BY itself: I planted it there, and (by now) it has grown to about 4 feet tall). So it is that God planted the seed of HIS LIFE in us (the Bible calls this a "new creature") . . . a LIVING creature . . . NOT an idea, or a concept, it's a Life! HIS Life, growing as all seeds grow . . . the tree of Life, inside me . . . growing . . . growing ME (the new creature), and as I grow, I want that other tree less and less !

The two trees both still exist, but I'm choosing the only good tree: the Tree of Life . . . aren't you?

Becoming . . . as a Little Child

Jesus told a guy named Nicodemus (I call him "Nicky") that the only way to see, or to even get into the Kingdom of God was (is) to be "born again" (from above). Later, (in answer to a question about who would be the greatest in the Kingdom of God), He called a little child over to Him, and then answered His disciples, "Unless you get converted and become as little children there ain't no way you will even GET INTO the Kingdom of Heaven" (my paraphrase) . . . hmmm

So, if I wanna both see and get into His Kingdom, there are TWO basic requirements: be born (in the spirit realm), and "become" as a little child. As Nicky said, "HOW in the world is THAT gonna happen?" (my paraphrase again)

OK so I am imagining that some of you are thinking something along the lines of "here he goes again . . . thinks he can actually answer those questions" . . . well, I AM gonna try to offer some thoughts that might give us some help here . . . but let me say right up front that if you are a person who likes to be thought of as a "spiritual giant", YOU WILL NOT LIKE THIS WRITING! Don't even bother to read any further! For whoever remains, let's tackle the "Born Again (from above)" thing first, OK?

For a couple of years now, I have been giving some attention to the development of an about 2-year-old lad. He is in many ways a very delightful guy, and I have watched him from when he was about 3 months old. When we were first introduced, he couldn't do much of anything; he COULD drink from a bottle with a nipple on it; he COULD lay on his back (or on his tummy if "Gram" insisted) (Gram is what many in these parts call my sister, who is taking care of this little fella a few days a week); anyhow, he COULD wave his arms and legs around in what appeared to me to be a very irregular manner (actually looked pretty much spastic to me); he COULD breathe; he COULD let everyone around know when things were not going like he wished (his lung-power was definitely "adequate"); and . . . of course . . . he COULD poop . . . BUT . . . all of this wondrous activity was AFTER he had been born . . . I have gotten ahead of myself here . . . for what happened leading up to his birth, I am going to have to rely on things that I have been told by quite a few others, and things that I have read, and a few ultrasound experiences that I have witnessed. I have become quite convinced that these are reliable sources. (otherwise I wouldn't be telling YOU) I'm only gonna talk about general stuff, cuz that's all I think I know, so here goes:

First of all I think it's important to recognize that "YOU" were not (FIRST of all) "YOUR" idea! (same for me, of course). Your Mommy and your Daddy had an idea of their own: that idea of theirs may or may not have included you, but during ONE of those experiences to which their idea led them, whether they knew it or not (at first), SOMETHING happened! . . . and that something was the beginning of you (and of course of me, too, but I don't want to keep saying it so for most of the rest of this writing, I'll just refer to "you" (and you will understand that I DO include myself in that "you"). So "you" were at that point begun. They call that "conceived". Do you think you were born yet? Didn't think so . . . you ain't THAT silly, are ya? but you DO exist, doncha ? yup . . . you . are . NOW . alive . . . a new being ! The thing that happened with your Mommy and Daddy was that Daddy's seed found and went inside Mommy's egg, and pow! There ya were!

It's about time, I think, to think about the fact that this is a picture (in the natural world) of how it comes about for you to be born again (from above). The stuff that happened with you when you entered human existence is a picture; a shadow of what happens to you in the spiritual kingdom. We are told that YOU are a NEW creature . . . a SPIRITUAL new creature . . . and that spiritual "new creature" which is YOU came about when your spiritual "Daddy" made loving contact with your spiritual "Mommy". The seed of your spiritual Daddy, Who is God Himself, found the spiritual egg of your Mommy, which is YOUR spirit (you who had been "living" on this earth for however many years) . God's seed + your spirit = YOU: the spiritual you; the you which is a new creation . . . from above, not from beneath.

Back to the natural, physical you. When Daddy's seed and Mommy's egg came together, at first there was an astounding, almost explosive growth and multiplication of life! shortly after that, you grew attached to the inside of your Mommy's "tummy", and before long that attachment grew to be the umbilical cord. This was very important for you because it was the only way to care for your physical development . . . so . . . you had this invisible power source within you, nudging you to do such things as grow all the parts or your body: you know, grow eyes and ears, and a tongue and fingers and toes and arms and legs and a stomach and all your interior parts like a backbone and kidneys and liver and heart and lungs, etc., learning to move your arms & legs and so much more. All this and more happened <u>BEFORE</u> you were born! It all went on inside Mommy's "tummy": all that growing! Mommy's tummy was absolutely necessary for all that, and normally this went on for around nine months . . . all this happened BEFORE you could be born . . . at that point you could neither SEE nor ENTER this world. But after a while, hopefully at the best time, that invisible power source (I'm sure by now you know Who that power Source is, doncha?) declared that it was time for you to be born, and so you were born into this world! YIPPEE!!!

Well you can see, I'm pretty sure, how important Mommy is to this whole process of bringing you to your birth, and of course you know it don't end there. Your poor Mommy has got a LONG time to go, cuz when you're born, yer not ready by any stretch of the imagination to master life on this earth. Mommy is the most important person in your life for many years to come . . . so I think we can see a little of what goes on before we get to be born.

But HOLD ON !!! That's for the physical "you": ain't there any mother for the spiritual New Creation which is you ? Yep, there IS ! . . . guess who? . . . It's YOU! YOU are the "Mommy" of that brand new spiritual "new creation"! Just like your natural earthly Mommy took care of you while you were inside her "tummy", being careful of things she ate, knowing how that would affect you too: like she had to be careful about her activities, knowing that even those would affect you, etc. etc. . . . Even so . . . YOU . . . are the one who will care for the development of that new creature growing within you. You will have to decide stuff like what sort of spiritual food you will eat; what sort of spiritual activities you will participate in, etc. etc.: All those choices, keeping in mind as much as you can the desire to produce a strong, healthy baby.

And after you were born, Mommy was the main one to help you get to where you could be called a "grown-up": changing your diapers; feeding you; cuddling you; helping you learn to walk; to talk; to count; to recognize colors; to potty-train; to eat with a fork; to have a sense of humor; to shovel the sidewalk; to take out the trash. I could go on and on (as I'm sure you know) but I'm pretty sure you get the idea, so anyhow, YOU are the primary one to be doing similar things for that new creature "you", after he/she has been born. Let's remind ourselves that this new creation now growing inside us is a SPIRITUAL creation . . . new to us . . . we ain't used to having no "creature" growing inside us: We ain't used to spiritual stuff of any sort, really . . . it's all new to us . . . but God had HIS idea. (remember how your Daddy and Mommy had THEIR idea ?) Well here you are, and God told you HIS idea (and you agreed, like your Mommy agreed with your Daddy). Now you're the spiritual Mommy of a new spiritual creature, up to birth and beyond.

Fortunately for YOU, God (Who is the Father of spirits and therefore the Father of your spiritual new creature) is always with you, always directing and giving power for the growth of that new creature from conception through maturity; showing you the stuff that's best for you to be about; giving you strength and ability to do whatever is needed. In THIS world, the new creature needs arms and legs and a mouth, etc. to be about everything for which he is destined, and YOU, dear heart, increasingly become those arms and legs, etc., and somewhere along the line, by attending to your new spiritual creature, that new one becomes you: the new you . . . and though it is possible for you to do stuff the way you used to, you just don't WANT that any more, most often! You gradually cease to think of yourself those ways: you used to think of yourself as alive, but now you see that you were in fact dead, and now, because of the new life in your new creature you have identified yourself with your new creature.

Of course on this earth your Mommy had some help every

now and then: before you were born and usually considerable help just after you were born, and throughout the several years between when you were born and when you were ready to take on the steering of your own life: through the years of your semi-independence, to your mostly independent years, and as long as she lives, she will to varying degrees still be your Mommy (though of course how she does that will be continuously changing). For the spiritual "New creature" many others will come along to help: teachers; friends; the Church; school; relatives of all sorts: all these will be properly helpful to the degree that they themselves are genuinely being directed by the Lord (that invisible power source)

Of course, that Invisible Power Source, it MUST be understood all along the way, is THE true source, both of YOU as you "Mommy" of this new creation, AND of that New Creation himself: the source not only of power but also of direction and instruction for both of you !

Well, we've painted a picture, or more likely a sketch of some similarities between natural growth and spiritual growth. The most important of these is what (Who) I have called the "Invisible Power Source". How both for the new creature and for you as the "mommy", HE is the One to be looked to and depended on . . . depended on continually . . . at all times . . . for every supply for every need . . . for every wisdom in every situation.

So we gotta become like a little child, right? In what ways? What do YOU think? Some of my thoughts follow:

1. - a little child is worry-free.
2. - a little child is confident in his/her fathers' care. (and in Mommys' care too)

3. - a little child is totally dependent on his/her parents for whatever he/she needs.
4. - a little child goes trustingly to his/her parents when hurt.
5. - a little child trusts what his/her Father (or Mommy) says.

These are only a few characteristics. I am sure there are many more you could mention, but as "spiritual Mommy" to the spiritual new creation growing inside you, what might you be about at times when that new creation is shaky: not able to live these things? Father is there at all times, doing everything that ONLY HE CAN do. It is Him, using ALL His resources to bring that new creature to maturity at all times and in all places and situations. HE will do His part without fail. But what can you (the Mommy) do, as you look to HIM? As you set out to follow HIS leading, dependent on HIM to lead you and empower you, that new creation will indeed become "the new you"! By taking your spot growing that "New Creation", the OLD you increasingly fades, and you BECOME that new creation (or, that new creation becomes YOU), which IS like a little child !

So (since you have grown to be big and strong and self-sufficient, etc.), HOW will YOU "become" as a little child? Big and strong and self-sufficient are NOT characteristics of the "new you", ya know: NOT characteristics of a little child . . . so I'm thinking if you wanna become as a little child (so you can see and enter the Kingdom of God, ya know) . . . I'm thinking you will have to begin to resist all those grandiose thoughts about how big and strong you are . . . and pay attention to the developing of the "New You". If you will do that, you will no longer be big and strong and self-sufficient: the "New Creation" will develop; He will become the new "You": and since the characteristics of that one include a constant recognition of his dependency all the time, everywhere, a knowledge of his Father's unlimited resources, and a conviction that his Father is totally good and is taking care of everything . . . because of that, he (you) WILL be like a little child, and you WILL both enter and see God's Kingdom !

Equal-ness

Yes, I know . . . the real word is equality . . . I did it on purpose . . .

When I searched for a definition of "equal" on the internet, I ran into some interesting stuff . . . such as that many of the sources used the word "equal" as part of the definition . . . now I was always told that it is a no-no to define a word by the same word . . . not allowed . . also, none of the entries seemed able to offer any meaning other than by linking it to something else . . . as Bob has written, "the concept of equality requires context" . . . so trying to wrestle with a satisfactory definition is a vain effort, like trying to grab a handful of air. The word "equal" (by itself) has no meaning . . . it's a "nothing burger" . . . there's no <u>THERE</u> there!

When I searched the scripture, I found nothing anywhere that declares (or even implies or suggests) that God (Who DOES create all things) . . . nothing to say or suggest that He created ANY THING or ANY ONE "equally". Jesus DOES tell us that we are worth many sparrows (now isn't that comforting?), and He has said a few more things that we'll talk about later.

Let's think about why we hang onto this idea (that we're all created equal): isn't it mostly that we don't like to think of ourselves as LESS than anybody else? To whom do we like to think we're equal? Billy Graham? The Pope? A favorite teacher or singer or preacher or doctor or lawyer or corporate exec, etc? How about the drunk staggering out of a bar? How about a septic tank worker? or a laborer on some construction site? a cab driver?, etc. I'm thinking we're not so keen on being "equal" to this last bunch, so personally, I'm thinking that our thinking is messed up about this matter! Isn't it true that we like to compare ourselves favorably with those we admire, but with those "others" what we actually tend to think is that we are BETTER than they are (NOT equal to them)? I'm thinking that mostly we think about how being equal will be to our advantage regarding some "right" or other that others have: a combination (as I see it) of FEAR that I will not get what I think I deserve, on the one hand, and on the other hand, PRIDE that "I am not like THEY are" . . . am I wrong? Tell me how, OK?

Let's think for a bit about things Jesus had to say . . . and other things that God said in the Scripture . . . Jesus taught that we were not to call anyone Rabbi (teacher), because HE is the Master and WE are all brothers (can you see the tendency here to elevate certain ones above others?) . . . this is not spoken to make us all equal, but rather to point out that we are all brothers . . . then going on, He tells us that if we wanna be great, we need to become servants (and that the greatest needs to be the servant of all). Me the servant, and others the served. Where does the question of equality come in here? And in all His talking about masters and servants, where is "equal-ness" spoken of by Him? In the "Sermon on the Mount" what is all the talk about how we are to order our lives with varied others about? Did He teach those things to say that we are all equal? When He tells us to take the LOWEST seat at the table is that because we are all equal? When He spoke about trying to take a splinter out of another's eye while I have a log in my own eye, is He thinking we are equal? Are the fallen angels equal to those not fallen? Is the leper equal to the blind man? Jairus' daughter equal to the woman with the issue of blood? Judas Iscariat equal to John? The woman who dropped a couple of pennies in the offering plate equal to those who sounded a trumpet when they gave? John the Baptist equal to all the other prophets? (Jesus didn't seem to think so, did He?) I could go on and on for quite a bit, but I won't, so relax !

How about all the differing gifts and ministries spoken about in <u>Romans 12</u> . . . <u>I Corinthians 12 – 14</u> . . . <u>Ephesians 4</u>? Talking about equality? I don't think so ! How about the instructions to submit to those who have the rule over you? Equality? Or submitting to all the "brethren" (and sistern) . . . how about the man being head of the woman, or the wife submitting to her husband? Equality? Even perhaps MORE specifically, "Let this mind be in you which was also in Christ Jesus, who did not think it a thing to be grasped to be equal with God (though He WAS God) — lowliness of mind — but emptied Himself, taking the form of a servant" Equality? Or Brother <u>Paul</u>, who wrote such things as "<u>don't think more highly of yourself than you ought to think</u>", or "<u>Consider others better than yourself</u>". Better? Not equal? Or <u>that those who compare themselves WITH themselves are not wise</u> . . . etc.

My personal thought is that we would be better off if we would eliminate all this "equal" stuff from our minds and our vocabulary . . . God created us all uniquely, with specific bents and talents and gifts and abilities unique to each, and He planted within us who are His, HIS VERY LIFE, which IS Love. We are all given to express THAT Life (agape) to everyone that touches us AS WE ARE (not like everybody else is) . . . NOT because everyone is "equal" . . . we are not! This Love recognizes (and glories in) the uniqueness (NOT the "equal-ness") of us all, so to sum it up, we were NOT all created "equal", and we are still NOT "equal". We are not "equal" to anyone who has ever lived, or ever will live, and my thought is that we oughtta give more attention to what God has said than to what ABE said or what is written in our national constitution. What we ARE is supremely, absolutely, and totally LOVED by God . . . Let's not be making any substitutes!

From The Rocker

So I'm sitting here in my big rocker, out on the porch one warm August evening, watching the sun set behind the big oak and listening to the crickets, occasional bird-tweets, and (every now and then) Mr. or Mrs. Gray squirrel voicing his or her annoyance at something or other . . . remember now, I'm IN my rocker . . . this is very important, because I KNOW <u>SOME</u> of you will be thinking, "he's off his rocker", which is NOT the case: I am IN it!

Anyhow, as I'm sitting here IN (got it?) my rocker, just enjoying the sights and sounds and the warm, gentle summer breeze, I'm hearing a tiny voice say "I hope you all realize just how important I am: my sister and I, we take ALL the air our human breathes in (we even make him able to DO that), and separate it so he gets the good part (which he calls "oxygen") and then we help him get rid of all the other stuff" . . .

Then I heard like a chorus of voices, some very high (which made me think they must be very tiny), some very deep and low (which made me think they were pretty big), and lots of others that sounded like they were somewhere in-between . . . They were singing something like this: "that IS important, Lovely Lung Sisters, but if you didn't have all of US to carry that good stuff to every single part of our human, tiny or huge, and then deliver it back to the pump so he could recirculate things, then what YOU do would not BE all that important . . . YOU . . . NEED . . . US . . . which makes US . . . VERY important"

"Well wait just a moment", I heard yet another voice say . . . rather deep and, I thought, rather kindly-sounding: "I am not just "a pump". You VAC* choristers sing very nicely, and you do your work very well, too, and without a doubt you are ALL VERY important, BUT . . . I am right at the heart of things, which is why I am called "Sir Big Heart", and I think that should be spoken of with a bit more respect. After all, without my continuous work for our person (several times a minute, 24/7, with no pause or even any rest, taking the stuff you bring me and faithfully, without fail, delivering it TO the Lovely Lung Sisters so they could do their part for our human, YOU ALL would be nothing but a bunch of flat, empty tubes running all around in our person . . . SO . . . you really (ALL of you) should definitely recognize that I . . . am EXTREMELY important".

"All that is very well and good", another voice said (smooth and very intelligent sounding), "but don't you all realize that it is ME that's REALLY important ? After all, it is I who run the whole show! I take in, and I process ALL the messages from every single part of our person; it is I who process it all, and then it is I who send out a responsive message to all 400 or more of you, letting you know what to do and when to do it all for the good of our person."

"True, true" . . . another chorus . . . high-pitched, and quite nervous sounding . . . "You are indeed very important, Sir Intel, but really, Sir, since WE are the ones who gather all the messages from all over our person and deliver them all to you . . . and then, once you have decided what messages you want to send, and where you want to send them, isn't it US who deliver them where you say (and don't we do it extremely fast?), shouldn't we be thought of as quite important too, even if we ARE a bit nervous?

And then I heard what sounded like hundreds or more voices, all talking at the same time but saying different things, and I could not understand ANY of it, though I had the feeling they all wanted everyone else to hear how important they were. This went on for some time as I sat there listening and trying to understand, IN (NOT OFF) my rocker.

THEN . . . THEN . . . the BIG voice . . . ALMOST knocked me OFF my rocker . . . almost, but NOT quite . . . "CHILDREN, CHILDREN", He said, 'WHAT in the WORLD are you TALKing about?

"Please, Sir", came another voice, (I THINK it was the right knee-cap),"we were just trying to figure out who's most important. There's more than 400 of us here in our human: how can we know who's most important?"

"Most important?", asked Big Voice, "you mean, which of you is more important than all the others? You sillies !!! I created you ALL: all 400+ of you, and I created ALL (EACH) of you for a specific purpose: don't you see? ALL of you are EXTREMELY important! Patrick, YOU, on your person's right knee (see I TOLD you it was the right knee cap) and your twin sister Patricia, on his left knee, BOTH are SUPREMELY important for protecting those knees . . . but neither of you are at all important for doing Sir Big Heart's job, or for doing Sir Intel's job either (although both of them DO help YOU do YOUR jobs) . . . I created THEM to do THAT . . . as a matter of fact, I created ALL of you (every single one) to do what you do to help all the others do what THEY were each created to do, all for the good of your human. Isn't that what makes each of you happiest, and most content? When you're busy doing what I created you for?

"Oh, I see !", said another (tiny) voice which I thought was the left pinkie-toe, "that means we're all equal !"

"Equal . . . Equal? . . . EQUAL-SCHMEQUAL!!!", said Big Voice. "NO ! . . . NOT equal . . . I don't create ANYTHING equal! Humans try to do that all the time, BUT I NEVER DO! I create all 400+ of you to be UNIQUE: UNIQUE, but NOT . . . EVER . . . EQUAL! and YOU . . . ALL . . . are VERY IMPORTANT !"

So then all the voices died down, and I thought all 400+ of them were considering what Big Voice had told them.

Well, this got me thinking (I do that quite a bit whether I am on or off my rocker, though by this time I am hoping you know that I am NOT OFF my rocker).

So anyway I was thinking about the Church, which the Book says is <u>Jesus'</u> body, with all of us (I think there are greatly more than 400+ of us) each being a part of His body, and I'm wondering if maybe . . . just maybe . . . WE might be all tangled up (like my voices), thinking which of US might be most important? (and which of us, we might be thinking, is really NOT all that important? Could it be that we are not so different from my "voices? . . . I wonder . . . What do YOU think ?

*-Vein, Artery, Capillary

This Mind part 1

"Let this mind be in you, which was also in Christ Jesus: Who, being in the form of God, thought it not robbery to be equal with God: but made Himself of no reputation, and took upon Him the form of a servant " (Philippians 2: 5 & 6. KJV)

So . . . just what IS this mind which we are supposed to "let be" in us? A few thoughts: first, Jesus knew He was God . . . He knew it and He declared it, and He also knew that this was a legitimate thing (He was in no way minimizing or stealing anything from God). That WAS Who He WAS, and He was absolutely right whenever He chose to reveal it. So what does that say about US, who are to let that mind be . . . in US? . . . I'm thinking one thing it means is that we are not to try to downplay or minimize who WE are (in Him, of course). Are you an Apostle? a Prophet? an Evangelist? a Pastor? a Teacher? . . . And what gifts has He given you? words of wisdom? words of knowledge? faith? gifts of healing? prophecy? discerning of spirits? working of miracles? tongues or interpretation of tongues? helps? governments? others?

Well it seems to me that whatever we have been given to be, or whatever gifts we have been given, "This Mind" accepts all of it without any sense of pride . . . it is simply a true acknowledgement of what IS. It is not stealing anything from God to acknowledge that I am (for example) a teacher. In OUR case, this kind of acknowledgement, far from stealing anything from God, actually glorifies Him (since all we truly ARE and all our spiritual gifts are FROM HIM, and not anything we have, apart from Him, attained) . . . so when we "let this mind" be in us we will first of all accept without pride or arrogance the truth of who we are and what we have been given.

Of course there is always the question of how truly we actually <u>KNOW</u> who we are, or what our gifts may be: that is a whole other question, and we will no doubt need to be corrected about those matters, but as we "Let This Mind be IN US", let's gratefully acknowledge who we are and what we have been given, best we can, and let Him give us whatever correction is needed.

"This Mind", however, though in no way diminishing Who He was (or who WE are) made Himself of "no reputation". So you are an Apostle? Great!!! Can you set aside that mighty reputation and help a neighbor in need? Help her clean her kitchen? Wash her dishes? without losing your "apostle-ship? Of course you can! That's the kind of thing "this mind" does, and in those times there is no need to declare your exalted "Apostle-ship". THAT simply stands as a truth of who HE has made you to be. HE WAS GOD, yet He washed His disciple's feet; instructed them continually; fed unruly crowds as only God-in-a-man could; walked dusty roads; made wine for a wedding party, etc., etc., all without saying "Look at Me . . . I'm God !". So if we "Let This Mind Be" in us, is there any need to declare ourselves as we go about simply being who we truly are? HE made Himself of no reputation: can we?. . . will we?

Then, He "took on Himself the form of a servant" . . . a servant! But let's pause a bit to think about this: to Whom was He a servant? Was it not ONLY GOD Whom He served? That is what He claimed, isn't it? (I only do what I see my Father doing" . . . and "the Words that I speak to you are not My

Own, but My Fathers'"). Of course He SHOWED that servant-hood through His acts and His speech while He walked this earth; healing all sorts of diseases; raising folks from the dead; teaching many about the Kingdom of God; walking on water to His disciples and caring for their distress: so very much more! "This Mind" cared for many needs . . . BUT . . . His service was, first of all, to His Father: NOT to the people!

So, when we "let this mind be" in us, OUR service . . . OUR subjection . . . OUR submission will ALSO be ONLY to the Father, will it not? Another scripture tells us that "we HAVE the Mind of Christ". We have no need to imagine it or to wish we had it or to try to act as if we had it. HE SAYS WE HAVE IT! . . . so . . . let's "let it be" . . . IN US!

This Mind part 2

OK . . . so now we are letting this mind be . . . in us . . . THIS MIND: you know, the Mind of Christ, WHICH WE HAVE! So, we are not, in any sense or to any degree denying or down-playing who we are in Him, or whatever gifts He has given us: we are setting our hearts to serve ONLY HIM, opening our hearts to Him so HE can do HIS works . . . through us . . . setting aside OUR reputation so HE can be seen and glorified.

So what does this LOOK like, you ask? What are we gonna be DO-ing? OK, I'll give you a taste (of the kinds of things this might look like): a list of things, mostly taken from "the Sermon on the Mount". This is only a taste, but it'll give ya a start.

So . . . THIS MIND . . . is poor in spirit, and has the Kingdom of God; mourns, and shall be comforted; is meek, and shall inherit the earth; hungers and thirsts for righteousness, and shall be filled; is merciful, and shall obtain mercy; is pure in heart, and shall see God; is a peacemaker, and shall be called child of God; is persecuted for righteousness sake, and has the Kingdom of Heaven; is reviled and spoken evil of (falsely) for Jesus' sake, and rejoices and is exceedingly glad because of the great reward in heaven; is the salt of the earth; the light of the world; does good works which glorify our Father in Heaven; does not break, or teach anyone else to break even the smallest commandment; is not angry with his brother without cause; does not look on a man (or a woman) to lust after them (does not commit adultery); does not divorce a mate; does not take oaths (says "yes" or "no" and stands by it); does not resist evil; turns the other cheek; gives more than what is demanded (goes the extra mile); gives to whoever asks; loves enemies; blesses those who curse; does good for those who hate, and prays for them; is perfect as Father is perfect; does not do good deeds to be seen by men (does them secretly, as though one hand doesn't know what the other does); prays in secret, without empty repetitions; forgives everyone for every thing; relies on Father for all needs; looks to attain treasure in Heaven (but not on earth); is single-focused (serves the Lord and does not serve "stuff"); doesn't worry about food, drink, clothing, etc. but trusts Father; seeks the Kingdom of God; is not concerned about the next day; does not judge (takes the log out of his/her own eye before trying to help another get the splinter out of their eye); is continuing to ask, seek, & knock, with the expectation of receiving; treats others the way he/she would like to be treated; enters the straight, narrow way to Life; is watchful for false prophets; DOES the Fathers' will (doesn't just listen to the words); serves and submits to Father only; in summary, THIS MIND . . . LOVES . . . as (like) Jesus loves us.

So . . . is this a good start? . . . ya want more? . . . well then, how about reading the four gospels (ya know, Matthew, Mark, Luke, & John), with a view toward finding out what and how Jesus taught; what He DID; what He said, etc. THAT IS "THIS MIND" (WHICH WE HAVE), in full color action.

STILL not enough? Then continue reading on through the book of Acts (THIS MIND in action in the early church) . . . and ya might as well continue reading on through the letters (you know, those letters written by Paul and Peter and James and Jude and John and whoever wrote the book of Hebrews). Then, of course, ya won't want to miss the book of revelation . . .

THEN . . . ya might wanna go back to the beginning (Genesis), where you can read how THIS MIND created everything that exists, and then on, of course, through the other books (the books of history . . . poetry . . . prophecy, etc.)

And THEN (or maybe just START HERE), take a good look around you: a REALLY GOOD look, at oceans; mountains; amber waves of grain; a blossom (an iris or a daisy or a petunia or a nasturtium or a bluet or an adder tongue or a jack-in-the-pulpit)! take a real' good look, and SEE . . . "THIS MIND".

THEN . . . look at the sky (the clouds; the sun (don't look at that directly, ya know); the moon and the stars; the milky way). Think about what we have learned about the universe! NOW, think about the invisible universe, out of which everything is composed: cells, molecules, atoms, electrons, protons, and neutrons . . . other, much smaller particles . . . and of course the invisible force that holds it all together and makes it all work. Got it? Got all that? Great!!!

THAT: all that and more is THIS MIND (which we are to "let be" in us). And the reason we <u>CAN</u> "let this mind be in us" is because . . . because . . . it <u>IS</u> . . . <u>IN US</u>! Pretty staggering, ain't it? I'm going fer it . . . you?

Communication

Now THERE'S something to think about! Didja ever? Think about it, I mean. I KNOW you've been trying to communicate ever since . . . well . . . at LEAST since you were in your mommy's tummy. Ya KICKED her when you were there, didn't ya? And then ever since ya got OUTTA her tummy you've been trying to communicate something or other. This much I know for sure, but I'm wondering: just how successful were you? Did she know what you meant when you kicked her? for that matter, did YOU know what you meant when you kicked her? And later, a few months after you left her tummy, you started making noises, almost all the time you were awake. I suppose YOU knew what those noises meant, but how about your poor mom? SHE didn't SPEAK that language, ya know . . . she TRIED to understand what you meant: sometimes I think she got it, at least partly. Most of the time she just guessed (since she knew you were trying to say SOMETHING !) A LOT of the time she just couldn't figger it out. Of course as time went on you began to understand HER language, and bit-by-bit the two of you got to where you understood each other (most of the time). But now I'm wondering, how good is your communication NOW . . . now that you've grown up . . . do ya ever have any problems trying to tell sumbuddy else what's on your mind? I'm thinking prolly you're considerably better at it than you were at first . . . so how come stuff just doesn't always get properly communicated these days?

Of course you know by now (as "they" tell us) that words are only a small part of what gets communicated: stuff like the expression on your face, and whether or not you cross your arms, or your legs, or whether you are leaning TOWARD or AWAY from them, etc., etc. ad nauseum (or almost) . . . and then of course there is your ACTIONS to be considered (my mommy used to tell me that my actions spoke louder than my words . . . and others have said something like "what you're doing talks so loud I can't hear what you're saying"). Such a complicated thing, communication! But WHY? I usually know perfectly well what I want to say. Don't you?

So that's my introduction. Now on to some thoughts, which are, of course, the main reason I'm writing about this (as I suspect you already know), so I'm thinking that maybe the MOST problematic thing about communicating anything is that it all starts with something like an idea; a thought; a wish, or a felt-need etc. And all those kinds of things are invisible: ya can't see 'em or hear 'em or touch 'em or taste 'em, or smell 'em, and we are used to seeing, hearing, touching, tasting, and smelling. So how do we get this thing that we can't absorb by OUR normal senses . . . this "invisible" something . . . how can we transform THAT kind of thing into something that some other person CAN see or hear or touch or taste or smell? There's the challenge of communication, as I see it !

So of course our task is to take that "invisible something" and shape it so we can convey it to others, and that is a skill that must be developed far beyond what I knew when I was in my mommy's tummy. And that, I think, is an on-going process all my life: "learning" how to shape that thing into something that has a chance of being understood by others. Hopefully we get increasingly good at that as we "mature".

But then there is ANOTHER issue: the other one has to somehow take the way we have presented something, and reverse the process inside themselves so they can hopefully get back to that "invisible" original idea or thought, etc. If they are able to do this successfully, then good communication has come about . . . great! But it seems to me that a great deal of the time stuff breaks down such that either my ability to present a thing or their ability to understand it is faulty: not sufficient for the task, and so the good communication we (probably both) WANT . . . fails. We haven't truly communicated. This, I think, is our typical human condition.

Fortunately for us, there is ANOTHER thing to consider which has to do with our human spiritual capacity: ya know how every now and then ya just "know" something, or ya can hear BEHIND what someone is saying or doing something that is really going on; something BEYOND the stuff we can see, hear, taste, touch, or smell, but somehow ya just "know" something which later is shown to be true . . .

And for those of us who have received Eternal Life, we have yet ANOTHER gift: we can understand things because the Lord shows us what is really going on, and what is behind what someone else is trying to communicate. That is a function of Eternal Life: <u>REAL Life</u>!

But now think about trying to convey to somebody else things about God: He is definitely invisible, right? And He is clearly "different" from humanity, isn't He? Don't I need to "learn" how to begin to understand Him? Isn't that an increasing ability, like learning human language? . . . and that ability in others . . . is that now also a growing thing? In the natural, long before I have any hope of mastering Algebra, I have to master much more basic things, such as 1-2-3's, etc. Do we think this is any less true in the Spiritual Realm? (think "Kingdom of Heaven")

So I'm thinking (yup, there he goes again) that both in the natural human level and in the invisible Heavenly realm . . . both realms . . . it is best by far if we can hold a gentle idea; a gentle perception of both our own abilities to communicate anything, AND the ability of others to truly absorb and understand what's being communicated. And also that the best "chance" (by far) of being able to either express or receive communication is when we have received Eternal Life, and depend on Him Who gave me that Life. My thought is that apart from that, there is no hope of good, accurate communication, except perhaps on a very surface, superficial level.

Well there is quite a lot more that could be said about this, as I'm sure you know, but this will have to do for now. These are (some of) my thoughts: What are yours'?

Communication . . a
Post-script to Teachers

Teachers, I'm thinking, have a somewhat unique set of challenges: for example, one Scripture says that not many of us oughtta be teachers cuz teachers will get "greater judgment". Another scripture says that if we DO speak, we should speak as the "Oracles of God". Yet another tells us that if we think we know anything, we oughtta acknowledge that we don't know ANYTHING . . . YET . . . as we ought. Now for someone who thinks he <u>IS</u> one of them teachers, this all feels a bit on the scary side: on the one hand we teachers have been "given" this "gift" that pretty much burns within us . . . Father has given us stuff to TEACH, for goodness sake! What the heck are we supposed to DO with it? But it HAS been given to us, so OBVIOUSLY we gotta do SOMETHING with it . . . but then on the other hand those scriptures FEEL pretty much like warnings, if you ask me. Of course I realize ya prolly did NOT ask me, but there ya have it anyway.

So I'm planning to letcha know some of what I think I know so far, OK? First, if we are teachers I think we might as well (prolly BETTER) settle it that THAT is what we ARE: a Teacher! So we get stuff . . . to TEACH, ya know . . . so I'm thinking we had best be getting ON with it, and do the best to be true to the stuff we've been given, all the while keeping in mind, best we can, the instruction (warnings?) we have ALSO been given.

One thing that might help here is if we bring back to our mind how very L—O—N—G it took US to gain this vast storehouse of wisdom we now possess: that we did not amass it all at once (or is that just ME?) It was built into us, I am thinking, one little bit at a time, from our foundation (we only have ONE of those, ya know) to the magnificent edifice we now are, and even that spectacular structure is designed and purposed to keep on increasing . . . Forever!

And that is how it is, with every cotton-picking one of us: not only us who are given to teaching, but for those, too, who Father has put in the place of HEARING the stuff He gave us to teach (and everybody else, for that matter).

We gotta keep in mind that THEY (just like us) are SLOW growers, so the stuff we're gonna pass along to THEM needs to be for THEM right where they ARE . . . wherever they ARE . . . in THEIR learning and growth. This great wisdom we have is FOR THEM (like just about EVERY gift). We have the "gift" to teach, but the stuff we are given TO teach is not, first of all, for US . . . FIRST, it is for THEM (though of course we always benefit, too).

So . . . whether we are using our teaching gift for several thousand folks, or for twelve, or three, or even one (as it was for Jesus), or whatever number, the target for the teaching is always "THEM": NOT for us to show off OUR growth or knowledge.

So let's us teachers . . . TEACH . . . whenever and however we may, keeping in mind that it is HIS message (HIS WORD) for HIS people and for HIS purposes, and let us be always depending on His Mercy toward us personally. We WILL blow it, ya know, since we are ALL afflicted with that thing called "pride". We ARE ALREADY forgiven for all of that, so let's press on to offer whatever we have been given . . . HIS Word, given to US . . . by HIM, for THEM . . . our gift is to be His conduit: blessed conduits to be sure. We are His Teachers: a wonderful thing!

Faith

Without faith it is impossible to please God . . . that's what HE said. He did NOT say "without faith it is impossible to be loved by God" (thankfully), just that we cannot PLEASE Him without it . . . so if we would like to PLEASE Him, perhaps it would be good to explore this thing called faith which we need to have if we are to please Him.

So . . . what IS faith? Scripture tells us it is "the substance of things hoped for: the evidence of things not seen". Both of these refer to something not yet in our experience: as another scripture says, if we have something (in Hand) there is no need for hope, because we can see it and handle it, and we have it; no need for, nor place for faith. So clearly the context for faith is in the realm where what we hope for is not yet visible or present to us.

So in that context where we have not yet experienced or possessed something for which we hope or pray, that which gives those hopes or prayers substance or evidence is faith: substance . . . evidence . . . what makes a thing real; weighty; not empty or wishy-washy: our faith!

Well then how do we GET this substance and evidence without which it is impossible to please God? Scripture says that it comes by HEARING, but hearing WHAT? And how CAN we hear? Cuz if we hear, then we have faith, right? And then we can please God, right? Well that same scripture goes on to say that hearing comes by the right-now-in-the-present-moment-spoken word of God: that is, it is God speaking to us right now who enables us to hear whatever He wishes to say to us and in whatever manner He wishes to say it. When He "speaks" to us, that Word of His ENABLES us to hear what He is saying: when we "hear", we know WHAT He is saying. And that same "word" carries the full power to carry out that "word" which He has spoken. When Jesus said to the man, "Get up! Take up your bed (mat) and walk, there was the instruction in it (get up, etc.); the causing of the man to be able to hear the instruction, AND the power to do what Jesus said . . . that whole package was in Jesus' word to that man. Even to Lazarus, who was physically dead, the right-then-spoken-word of Jesus carried the power to make that dead man hear what He said, and also the power to DO it: God's Word; His power to cause hearing; His enlightening to bring understanding; His strength and ability to carry out that Word . . . and us??? we hear it; we believe it in our hearts; we set out to agree with it and to DO it, ALL with HIS strength. He does everything: we "accept"; we "believe"; we "do it" . . . all because of all that's included in His "word", and then we please Him . . . hmmm . . . not really all that difficult, is it?

But there are a couple of aspects to faith: first, and basic to all, there is TRUST: a heart-felt conviction based on what He has already revealed to us of His nature; how He IS; what His character is; how He normally acts; what kind of Father He is, etc. (rather general in nature) When scriptures "come alive" to us, this is the kind of revelation that helps us to understand these more general things: how He is able to do stuff that is far beyond our thoughts; how He will take care of whatever we give Him to care for; how He will give us peace in the midst of things that tend to make us anxious; how He is dedicated to caring for us in all the aspects of our personal lives; how He knows what we need before we ask Him; what we can expect from Him when we are giving; how He causes ALL THINGS to work together for good, etc., etc. When we have heard these things, and "come into line" with them, by His grace and His power, then we please Him. If not, we will have failed to please Him though we have not in any way diminished His love for us. These are things on which to base our TRUST; our confidence in His nature; in How He is.

Then there is the aspect of belief: when He tells us something specific, such as Abraham, when God told him that "next year about this time Sarah will conceive and bear you a son" . . . or when He tells you to make a meal for sister Hannah, or to stop and pick up a gallon of milk on your way home, or to pick up that piece of trash over there, or to lay hands on that man because I want to heal him, or to call sister Sally back from the dead, or whatever . . . this is where the belief aspect of our faith enters the picture: by His Word He has caused us to hear; enabled us to understand; and empowered us to do it: and that pleases Him.

Of course it is unlikely that we would be able to believe Him regarding a specific thing unless we have at least begun to develop a heart-felt knowledge of His character: how could we begin to trust someone we do not know? And why would we want to be obeying such an one? But for those of us who are His children, He has already begun to reveal Himself, and He will continue to do that throughout the course of our lives, so that we shall be able to . . . increasingly . . . please Him.

His Word can come to us in many ways. We have largely been taught that He speaks to us through His scriptures, and this is, of course, true, provided that His Holy Spirit is causing that scripture to come alive to us in the now. But also (as scripture declares) the heavens speak His Word to us; all creation is His

Word to us (it becomes life to us when He causes it to do so in the present). The prophet can speak His Word to us, as can any other human being. in one recorded instance even a donkey spoke from Him, and of course He can and does speak to us directly in our hearts.

So the "steps" of faith are from hearing, to understanding, to doing . . . all the steps: hearing, knowing, and doing are essential if faith is to be full. To miss any part of that is to miss faith, and therefore to miss pleasing God. BUT He is at work within us, both to will, and to DO His good pleasure: HE is at work to cause us to please Him . . . Fantastic News!!!

I suppose it would be well to be sure to emphasize the place of "obedience" in these steps. I suppose, for example, it would seem good if we "heard" and "understood" that He said, "_be anxious for nothing, but in all things by prayer and supplication, with thanksgiving, let your requests be known unto God, and the peace of God which surpasses all understanding will guard your hearts and minds_", and of course having His peace seems mighty nice. Yet if we do not actually let Him know our requests by praying and even "supplicating", then the peace that would follow will not be ours; our sense of "hearing and understanding" will have been useless; empty; vain. We will not have acted in faith; not have pleased our God. If, however, we DID do those things, our faith is complete, and we will have pleased Him. No amount of simply hearing and thinking we understand can please Him, for then we have blocked what His word was intended to accomplish, and that, of course, cannot please Him: only carrying it through (always in His strength) can complete His intended purpose, and be pleasing to Him.

But what about when we don't HAVE any sense of "word"?; when we strongly feel the need for some sort of direction? We feel we need to do SOMETHING, but no clue about what to do . . . what THEN? This is when we walk in the FIRST aspect of faith, that of TRUST. We rely then on His character; on HIS ability and desire to direct our steps in the way in which we are to go. We <u>DON'T</u> know, so we <u>TRUST</u>, and that is faith in action, and it pleases Him.

So . . . when do we KNOW? When do we RECEIVE the "end" of our faith? Did He tell us when? If so, we will know and receive THEN. Did He NOT tell us when? Well then we will have to wait "in faith" until whenever that "when" is. When God told Abe that about this time next year Sarah will conceive and bear a son, after around three months he made love to his wife, and about nine more months later, there the son was! But when He told Abraham that "in your Seed shall all nations of the earth be blessed", that is something that old Abe is still waiting to "see". He waits "in faith", pleasing God . . . and it's pretty much like that with us today!

A few "add-ons"

Faith as a grain of mustard seed: let's NOT focus on the SIZE of the seed: a mustard seed "Hears" the word of the Lord and, though it is indeed very small, it becomes a large plant, in whose branches birds can roost. The mustard seed "hears", submits itself to the authority and power of the One Who will cause it to grow, and consequently it grows. That's the kind of faith a mustard seed has, and if we had THAT kind of faith . . .

Faith is response: God is initiator, empowerer (is that a word?), finisher

Faith . . . when it's there, it is clear evidence that we have heard from God (it comes by hearing); that we have stepped into the stream issuing forth from the unseen Kingdom, which always accomplishes what it was sent forth to do. Its existence will be made clear when we act in accordance with what we have heard.

Good News About Bad Choices

So . . . 35,000 . . . That's how many choices (decisions) "they" say we make, on the average, during a typical day . . . 35,000 . . . hmmmmmm . . . so I've "been a Christian" about 65 years, so you'd think I would have made 35,000 CHRISTIAN decisions each day of those 65 years: (you WOULD THINK that, wouldn't you?) If my math is correct, not counting leap years (check it out yerself), 365days -x- 65 years -x- 35,000 decisions (choices) = Eight Hundred-Thirty Million, Three Hundred-Seventy-Five Thousand choices I have made in that time, "as a Christian"; and every day now I add about another 35,000 of 'em. Of course, most of those are sub-conscious choices, but that still leaves a huge number of conscious ones.

Some of those choices were (I hope) "good" ones. Others, I was not sure about: I just tried to make good decisions based on what I thought I knew, or what I thought was best. In retrospect, these might either be shown to be good (like I thought) or maybe not so good, or in retrospect I STILL might not know for sure which it was. And then there were the OTHER choices: ones I made without thinking about either what God thought or what was really good for anyone else; choices I made just to please myself, just because "I" wanted to do or say something. In retrospect, when I've been willing to take a real look at those choices, these have always been shown to be wrong; bad; harmful, etc.

So most likely I have made some good choices which, because they were "good", had "good" consequences. Some I hoped were "good" turned out to actually BE good, with good consequences also. These good choices were not a problem because, of course, the consequences were good. Some I hoped would be "good" turned out to be NOT good, so the consequences were bad, and of course those I made out of selfishness were not good either, so the consequences of those choices were not good . . . so . . . some good choices resulting in goodness, and other bad choices resulting in badness (is that a word?), but ALL of 'em are now in my past, and I can't do anything about it: no way to "un-do" any of those bad choices, OR their consequences . . . OUCH!

But there IS good news about this last bunch of choices (the BAD ones, ya know) . . . this good news is that Jesus has paid the price of ALL my bad choices: all of 'em, NONE excluded! All my bad choices (decisions) HE calls "sin", and by dying in my place, HE has paid the penalty for every bad thing in my life!

Another big piece of good news is that He can take ALL my choices, both "good" and "bad", and make them turn out for good in the end. How does He do that? I don't know HOW, only that He DOES it!

Another very good news-piece is that He LOVES me totally; unreservedly: when I make a "good" choice, or when I make a "bad" one. No less love when I make a "bad" choice, and no MORE love when I make a "good" one. How do ya figger THAT?

So this good news stands true for me with ALL my choices, and all I gotta do is BELIEVE! "Believe WHAT"? you ask . . . well . . . believe that Jesus came to die for my bad choices (sins) (this, of course implies that I know I HAVE sinned (made bad choices which had bad consequences, hurting other people) and believe that by Him dying I have been totally forgiven for every bad decision (choice).

Of course if you DON'T believe there is such a thing as "sin"; if you DON'T believe that you personally have sinned, so you think you don't need a savior, or if you DON'T believe that Jesus CAME to die for YOUR sins (bad choices, decisions), and therefor refuse His offer: if you DON'T believe, then I don't have any good news for you.

But that is not you . . . is it?

Grace

What IS Grace? How well do we understand it? Do we really NEED to understand it? Is it just another theological word, for theologians and preachers to know about? Or can we just simply understand it from its present-tense usage (you know, "she walked gracefully across the room", meaning that she didn't stagger, use an exaggerated stride, etc., or "she treated her guests with grace and dignity", etc., meaning that she spoke kindly to them or treated them nicely). Is that what it's all about? Or is there, thinking as a Christian, something much more; much deeper; much more important for us to grasp?

Many of us who are Christians have heard it taught that grace is "unmerited favor", or "getting what we don't deserve". Both of these statements are true, but they are lacking in depth if we are to truly understand God's grace toward us.

Ephesians 2:8--10, KJV says, "*by grace are ye saved, through faith . . . and that not of yourselves: it is the GIFT of God . . . NOT of works, lest any man should boast. For WE ARE HIS WORKMANSHIP, created unto good works which HE has before-ordained that we should walk in them.*"

Let's focus on the words "gift"; "not of yourselves"; "not of works" . . . Could we safely and truly say that WE are not the first cause of anything God does for us? Jesus said that no man comes to the Father except the (Holy) Spirit draws him; that He is the way, the truth, and the life, and that no man comes to the Father but by Him. Another scripture says that the heart of a man devises his way, but the Lord directs his steps; and another that the steps of a good man are ORDERED BY THE LORD. So what is our place in all this? Might it not be along the lines of just RECEIVING whatever He is giving, with no thought about whether or not I deserve that thing?

It seems to look like God thinks He should be the originator of everything; that whatever He does is because of His own plans and purposes; that it really doesn't matter what OUR understanding of things is; that HE is the only One that really understands everything, and knows how to work it all out, and that none of it is done because of our own counsel and "wisdom" . . . or "goodness" . . . or even BECAUSE OF our genuine obedience to Him: not BECAUSE of anything which is of us.

There is, of course, the matter of His discipline, or His correction in our lives: we need the discipline, or the correction, and of course there is the matter of our continuous need for direction: but is it US who dictate what that direction or correction or discipline, etc., will be? Sometimes we find ourselves thinking that way: yet even in this area it is actually HE who decides all of it, based on HIS knowledge of what is needed at this point in my "walk" with Him, as well as at ALL points of that "walk".

One scripture says that the GRACE of God has appeared unto all men, teaching us that, denying earthly desires, we should live soberly, righteously, and Godly in this present age . . . So . . . God is not obligated to teach us these things, yet He does. Is that important to us? Can we not just do whatever we want because we are not under law, but "under grace"? Do we really need to be instructed to deny our earthly desires? It is important that we understand that His Grace is not to be understood to mean that we can do just anything we please, and He will say it's OK. If something we are inclined to do is harmful (to ourselves or to others) we NEED to know this; and out of His goodness, quite CONTRARY to our desires and not in any way BECAUSE of those desires, He TEACHES us what we need to know.

So many of God's children go about their lives today with a deep, though usually unspoken sense that we can never measure up to whatever God "expects" from us and so therefor they really never count on the full wonder of His love for them personally. They could NEVER deserve it, they think, and of course that is actually true: they could NOT EVER deserve it. This is exactly the point of grace: being freely offered what they could NEVER earn or deserve. They can never deserve it, but they MAY freely HAVE it.

So, from the beginning it has always been and always will be God's grace freely extended to everyone . . . anyone who is willing for it to be that way may have all that God freely offers. While we were enemies, scripture tells us, Jesus died for us, paying for our sins and opening the access to our Father where our sin had caused our separation . . . While we were His ENEMIES!!! . . . so by His grace He reconciled us who were separated, and by His grace He gave us His Life and by His grace we are now His children: and as our Father, continuing in His grace, we shall be raised up into maturity; by His grace we shall be continually trained, directed, corrected and disciplined. HE, our Father; we, His children. His Grace, NOT our deeds! Let us grow in the GRACE and knowledge of Him.

So . . . grace . . . one of the characteristics of AGAPE (God) in which HE, when the times are right, brings or allows to be brought to all (every person or situation) everything that is good and needed to sustain all and to bring all to the fullness and completion of all, according to HIS design and purpose for all, without regard for who does or does not deserve it, or whether any thinks it is, humanly speaking, "good" or "bad". It will be shown to be goodness, freely and unrelentingly bestowed.

The Other Side Of Grace

It seems to me that when most of us think about the word "Grace", we're thinkin' 'bout all of the "good" stuff God gives us when we clearly and certainly don't deserve any of it . . . and I'm thinkin' that certainly IS Grace. So many things He has given us; provisions He has made; life, itself; air to breathe, and lungs for breathing it; all our five physical senses by means of which we can participate in our life in this world; the world itself, with all its beauty and grandeur; the beauty and intricacy of a blossom, an iris blossom, for example: and these are only a very small beginning of a list of all we have been given, totally without us earning or deserving any of it ! And of course there are the things of the Spirit: the invisible things like love and kindness and mercy, and then the matchless gift of eternal life, made possible through the death of Jesus, in payment for all our sins!

But there is another "side" of His Grace: this is the side we don't like so much, though from God's perspective it also is good which we haven't earned and don't deserve. I'm talkin' about such things as discipline, for example . . . no child likes to be disciplined, including us, God's children . . . it just ain't fun, and it don't feel good; or pruning for another example . . . ever been pruned? it never felt good to me . . . He cuts something off and it feels like part of ME is gone (which of course it IS). Then there's the grace that teaches me to deny ungodly desires . . . (Deny my OWN desires?) . . . yup . . . then there's the teaching that we gotta go through tribulation if we're gonna get into His Kingdom. (Tribulation? Really? What kinda Kingdom IS this, anyway?) Then He says we shouldn't think it odd when we go through various kinds of tests, trials, and even persecutions. The guy who wrote "Amazing Grace" said "it's grace that taught my heart to fear". Now I'm not sure about you, but these things don't seem very nice to me . . . they're HARD when I'm going through 'em, and I DON'T LIKE 'EM. I CERTAINLY did NOT ask for 'em, and I don't think I deserve 'em (well OK, I prolly DO deserve some of 'em), but in any case they didn't appear in MY life because I WANTED them to . . .

Yet with regard to ALL these kind of things, HE said they are ALL for my good: HE said all this negative, painful stuff would produce good stuff in me: stuff I NEED in order to become the best ME I could be; things that will cause me to become a well-functioning, grown-up member in HIS Kingdom. He even said we oughtta be full of joy: exulting and triumphing when we're going through this stuff (now THAT sounds counter-intuitive to me, unless . . . UNLESS I can begin to understand that all this stuff which seems and appears so BAD is in truth VERY,VERY good! Only then, I think, can I become very, very grateful: if I could see it with HIS eyes, I would be.

So God gives us many good things, (which we agree are good things) just because it's HIS nature (not BECAUSE OF what we have earned or deserved), and He ALSO gives us many other things WHICH ARE GOOD (but which, at least at first we DON'T think are good) also just because it's His nature: stuff we like, and stuff we DON'T like. BOTH are for our good, whether or not we know it or agree with it, and BOTH are His Grace . . . because HE loves us, and wants for us ONLY that which is good!

GRACE: Two sides (it appears) . . . both good . . . THAT'S HOW HE IS!

Growing

I got "saved" over 60 years ago, and stayed in that church from then until I left for college about 8 years later. In those early years I learned a lot about God, and a lot about what my life as a Christian oughtta look like. I am still grateful for much that was given me in those years. Since those years, however, there have been quite a number of things that I "learned", that I have needed to "unlearn", and I am still unlearning (as well as learning).

One of those things I have had to unlearn has to do with our salvation: I do not know whether or not that church actually taught this, but somewhere along the way I developed the notion that we start our Christian life by "getting saved" (by "accepting Jesus as my Savior", or "inviting Jesus into my heart", or by praying the "sinner's prayer", etc., etc.). . . . After that, we got through this earthly life until we died and "went to Heaven" to be with Jesus forever, where everything would be wonderful non-stop, never ending. We would have a glorious mansion there, made out of silver and gold, etc., and if we loved, say, bing cherries here on earth, we would have 'em in Heaven, only better bing cherries . . . and we would have EVERYTHING in Heaven that we loved here on earth, only much better there. So a lot of attention was given to the beginning, when we "got saved", and to the ending, when we finally made it through all our struggles, strife, pain, injustices

(I think most of us were taught that we just needed to hang in there until Jesus took us home and this horrible life would finally be ended). Not very much was taught us (at least in MY memory) about those in-between years . . . so . . .

I'm thinking that most of this "understanding" is at best, faulty, some of it totally untrue . . . all that aside for now . . . in this writing I'm hoping to think about that stretch of our life before we "go to heaven", and after we "get saved". Certainly there was a time in our lives when we heard about Jesus and believed in Him. According to Jesus, when we believed, we entered a reality where we would not die, but rather have a Life that goes on forever.

Eternal life . . . LIFE . . . what about this "Life" thing? What do you think? Does life just sort of hang around until someday it comes to an end and dies, or isn't Life quite another sort of thing? I've never personally seen a baby who was born and then just stayed a baby for 80 years and then died . . . have you? . . . Nope, they all grew, didn't they? (some grow only physically, but when we see that, we all know something's wrong;and yes, some do not show much growth spiritually, and whenever we see that, we also know something's wrong).

And so it is with all of us who have received that eternal Life: it's designed to grow. Isaiah 9:7 seems to say to us that we're gonna continue growing . . . forever! . . . all through our human life, our new spiritual life is destined to grow, and after our bodies die and we "go to heaven", we're just gonna keep on growing, permanently . . I gotta say, that's pretty hard to wrap my head around, but that's what HE says!

So anyway, let's take a look at a few scriptures that have something to say about this "growing" thing . . . in no particular order:

Peter tells us we oughtta go for what he calls "the sincere

milk of the Word" *in order that we would grow by it* . . . and later, he tells us to *grow in the grace and in the knowledge of the Lord*. . . (I Peter 2:2 and II Peter 3:18, KJV)

Paul talks about how those believers "ought to have become mature and spiritual, but they were still fleshly; carnal; and unspiritual (they had not grown). As an aside, this points us to the fact that it is possible for us not to grow as we ought) . . . (I Corinthians 3:1-3, KJV)

The writer of Hebrews echoes this thought, saying those believers "ought to have become teachers by now *(they had not grown),* but instead they needed to be taught again the basic things of the faith . . . (Hebrews 5:12-14, KJV)

Talking to the believers in Galatia, Paul tells us that those believers had started out well . . . in the spirit, and by the Spirit . . . but they had allowed themselves to be deceived by bad teachers into going back to the things of the law: *not only had they not grown, but they had gone back*: back to doing stuff in their own strength, etc. (Galatians, chapter 3 through chapter 5). Another pitfall to be watchful about; but this scripture shows us that *the normal "expectation" is that we grow* . . . out of our familiar flesh ways, under the law, INTO the Life of the Spirit, empowered by God.

To the Corinthian believers Paul explains that what's happening is that we are being transformed *(Growing)* out of the glory of the old system of laws into the much greater glory of the realms of the Spirit . . . day by day, as we gaze upon Jesus (IICorinthians 3:6-18)

Paul also says to his Ephesian brothers that we (all believers) *Are being grown together into a Holy Temple, in which God will dwell.* (Ephesians 2:20-22) . In another place (Ephesians 4:11-16) he tells them that God has gifted certain men, such as Apostles, Prophets, Evangelists, Pastors, and Teachers, and has given them to the church (us), <u>*to help us grow up*</u>: to equip us so we will not remain children, but will rather grow up into Christ, with the understanding <u>*that we will be able to help one another grow.*</u>

Well, these are a few scriptures that speak to us about the reality Of growing. It is expected that we WILL grow: it is normal; natural; even certain (if it is not blocked). You could no doubt find a bunch more scriptures, but let's first of all settle it that we're gonna grow; we're destined to grow . . . but how? in what ways are we gonna grow? Let me share a few ways I've thought about, in no particular order:

We need to keep in mind that we are not talking here about improving our "old man": remember, HE is already dead, and we have been born again . . . a spiritual birth . . . from above . . . our "new man". Yes, we ARE growing, but it is our "new man" that is growing . . . so . . . we are growing

1. - from being conceived to becoming a mature son.
2. - from this world, governed by laws and empowered by us to God's Kingdom, empowered by God.
3. - from being self-oriented to being God-oriented.
4. - from dependence on human ability and ingenuity and strength to absolute, never flagging dependence on God for direction and instruction and ability and strength.
5. - in our ability to live in and express God's Life (which is Love . . . Agape Love).
6. - from weakness to strength. (because of our increasing dependence on God for everything)
7. - in our ability to see (things, people, God) as they really are.

8. - in our desire for things to go God's way rather than our own way (progressing from grudging acceptance to fervent desire.

9. - in hearing God . . . to hungering to hear Him.

10. - in our experience of peace (rest), because we are also growing in our true knowledge of God; His Love (agape);His constant care for us; His unlimited power; etc.

11. - from acting out of our "old man" to manifesting our "new man".

I'm sure you will think of many other aspects or our growth, but for the purpose of this writing I'm hoping that it will help us flee from that idea that once we "get saved" there's nothing left to do except to grind our way through all of life's many hardships until we finally die and "go to heaven". Nope, that ain't it.

We got plenty o' growin' to do!

Growing Pains

Most of us have either experienced or known somebody who has experienced growing pains . . . as you know, these periods of life were definitely NOT pleasant. For me personally, it was quite a period of life when my knees . . . HURT . . . I grew to be 6'-5" by the time I reached 14 years: things got stretched, and especially my knees were painful. That's MY "growing pain" story: what's yours?

Anyway, this "growing pain" thing is a reality in our spiritual Life also. Of course we don't feel these in our physical bodies (usually), but we definitely DO feel 'em! WHERE do we feel 'em? It's pretty interesting to think about: we are, you see, a "new creation". From the moment when we believed on Jesus, this new creation sprang into existence. Eternal Life began for and in us, but this new creation did not "pop on the scene" fully grown, ya know . . . nope . . . it arrived as a seed. <u>THE</u> seed, destined to grow. And where is it gonna grow? . . . hmmm . . . well, this seed was planted INSIDE ME, so it's gonna grow right there inside me!

The problem is that in order for the new me to grow, it's the old me (not the physical part of the old me, but the inner part of the old me) that feels the pains. John the Baptist said at one point, speaking of Jesus, "<u>He must increase and I must decrease.</u>" I'm thinking this is a good picture of what is to happen with us: the Life of the new me is, in fact, Jesus. HE.IS.

OUR.(new creation) LIFE! That Life is gonna grow, and when it does, it's gonna push out the "old man" life. There's not room for two bosses in my newly created Life. When our new Life pushes out from inside, the "Old life has gotta go ! To put it bluntly, WE GOTTA DIE . . . and that's where the pain comes in.

The early apostles taught those early believers that it is THROUGH TRIBULATION that we enter the Kingdom. The Kingdom: Yup, you know, the Kingdom: the realm where God calls ALL the shots. Yep, I said ALL the shots: in that Kingdom we do not call ANY shots. God is in charge of <u>EVERYTHING</u>, and we are not in charge of ANYTHING in His Kingdom . . . ah, there's the rub . . . things just cannot go on any longer with us in charge . . . PAIN !!!

So . . . tribulation . . . what's THAT? Well, with the apostle Paul it involved a "thorn in the flesh" which God chose not to remove; being stoned with stones until they thought they had killed him (didn't work, of course); being beaten with rods and lashes multiple times; being thrown into prison; being shipwrecked several times; being bitten by a poisonous snake; being betrayed by his countrymen and forsaken by his co-ministers, etc., etc. Paul said that these kinds of things happened to him to enable him to stop trusting in himself and to begin trusting in the One who brings life outta death!

In my own personal life (in the last dozen or so years) it has involved (among other things) losing a business that seemed to be starting to be successful; having a stroke that to this day continues to have negative effects in a good portion of my physical body; taking a fall that damaged my vocal mechanism so I can no longer sing; being divorced, losing a wife and a home and much else; surgery for a cancer in the colon, and later, when they found another one, radiation and chemo for that one; heart attack; etc., etc. Through these, I have learned somewhat of what Paul learned, and have grown in my knowledge of the Lord in the process.

So there are a couple of examples: you have your own story, don't you? All of us who belong to Him have a story. So there's a happy ending to those stories . . . BUT . . . there is also PAIN, isn't there? Two things are happening: First, we grow; Second, we die (that is, when we grow (new man) we die (old man). Another way to say it is that when we die we make room for the new man to grow; to come forth! for me . . . and for all of you!

Hebrews 12:5-11 is interesting: chastening! I've never seen these verses pasted on anybody's refrigerator . . . and the Bible clearly says that this is NOT joyous, but grievous . . . BUT . . . afterword, wonderful stuff! I think this chastening thing is mostly related to God getting us away from some habit we have which we love, but which is actually hurting us; grievous; painful growing pains . . . BUT . . .

How about being on the Potter's wheel? (Jeremiah 18:4) being smashed down onto His wheel: losing everything we thought we were and being re-shaped into some other thing which we don't know about; something entirely different. Ouch! . . . PAIN!

And how about that "pruning" thing? (John 15:2+) He said that for those of us who ARE bearing spiritual fruit (check out Galatians 5:22&23): again, those who ARE bearing fruit: He's gonna "prune" us so we'll bear MORE fruit! What? I thought I was doing pretty good with the fruit thing, but no . . . I gotta bear MORE . . . I gotta be pruned . . . PRUNED ! . . . do you know what that FEELS like ? Cutting stuff OFF; cutting parts of ME off; stuff I thought was GOOD ! Oh no . . . there I go again, eating some of the fruit of that tree (you know, the tree of the knowledge of good and evil). But it HURTS !

Of course there's the stuff that we can read about in <u>Luke 9: 23&24</u>, where HE said that if anybody wants to follow Him (that's me, and I'm thinking it's you too) . . . anyhow, if we're gonna follow Him, we gotta turn away from OUR OWN WAYS of doing things (even our own ways of thinking) . . . ME? . . . turn away from ME? . . . from MY ideas of how things should go? . . . from MY judgments of stuff? . . . HOW IN THE WORLD? Then He says that we gotta take up our cross, every day. Our cross? The thing I hang around my neck or the thing on the top of our steeple? How? He's talking about the thing they KILL people on? We're talking about DYING here . . . so we're back to the "dying thing . . . I HATE that ! But then He goes on to say that if we DON'T carry that thing around we're gonna lose. Lose what? He says we'll lose the stuff we've been hanging onto: the stuff we thought was our life?

Yup, that's what He said: either we let it go willingly, or it will be taken from us later. (if we want His Kingdom, of course) Let it go or have it taken: such a deal, right? . . . BUT . . . there IS one good part of this deal. IF we will lay down what WE think is our life, THEN we WILL get what HE KNOWS <u>IS</u> our life! Now really, if ya think about THAT, it really IS a fantastic deal! Of course there is still that pain we gotta go through: another growing pain!

Then there's the "caterpillar/butterfly" kind of pain . . . Did you ever go through a time when you had absolutely NO idea who you are, or what's happening, or where you're going? I have, and for me, that is PAINFUL. When a caterpillar builds his chrysalis round himself, he can't go nowhere; he's imprisoned; stuck. Does he know WHY? What he's gonna become? Soon, he turns into a shapeless what? A chrysalis filled with a very colorful LIQUID: no shape at all, unless you count the shape of his chrysalis! Does he know? WE know what he will become, but does he? I don't think so, but of course I've never spoken with one, so ??? But I DO know what it feels like not to know! Not to know anything . . . PAIN!

This typifies us at many points of our spiritual development (growth). We are in touch with most of the outward things, like the time we first believed in Jesus (many of us called this "getting saved"); when we were baptized in the Spirit; healed or experienced some other miracle; when we were "ordained" to our ministry; etc., etc.

BUT . . . in between those times . . . as at ALL times, God is growing us in ways we cannot see or understand. It's like a very young infant, growing: we see him the day he was born, but before he was born, invisibly to us, a great deal of growing was happening. Then, right after he was born we got to witness certain events: he started breathing; crying; nursing; pooping; waving his arms and legs around; then he rolled over; then sat up; then crawled; stood up; walked; talked: on and on, special events that many moms mark on their calendars. Yet all along throughout and in between these events, there's a whole lot o' growing going on, which we have no way of observing.

So we can see the outer stuff but not the inner stuff: Paul tells us that God is at work IN us (inner stuff), first of all to WANT to do things HE is choosing for us, then to actually DO those things (outer stuff). But since we are so used to thinking that we know how life should be happening, and since we can see only the OUTER stuff, we have a very hard time accepting the need for inner stuff to happen before the outer stuff <u>CAN</u> happen. If ya stop to think about it, ya know that it's NECESSARY for a young child to wave his arms and legs around in seemingly random movements, in order for him to have his muscles sufficiently developed to even try to roll over or sit up or crawl or walk. The inner, HIDDEN stuff MUST take place: it is this INNER stuff that makes the outer stuff even POSSIBLE! WITHOUT THE INNER STUFF, THERE COULD BE NO OUTER STUFF!

For a worm to become a butterfly, it MUST go through the "purely liquid" stage: no form; no shape. BUT by means of that INNER life, the worm life is ended and the butterfly life is formed and developed. For us humans, as God brings us from one level of life to another: in that phase LIFE IS GOING ON, though we don't (cannot) know what's happening to us (in us), and for us, that is painful: another growing pain . . . one of several!

Well, I guess I've spent quite a bit of time on this "caterpillar-butterfly" pain: as I see it, this particular pain (not knowing or being able to figure stuff out) . . . THIS pain is a component of all the other pains we've looked at, and I've become certain that the only way to overcome THAT pain is to learn not to trust in ourselves and our abilities and ideas (we all have 'em, ya know); but rather to trust in THE ONE Who brings Life outta death: OUR life, outta OUR death! Increasing trust (in Him) = decreasing pain!

OK . . . so these last two (the "not knowing" thing and the "dying to ourself" thing", these are the major pains we experience as we grow in the spirit. We are growing into the Kingdom of God (the realm where God rules everything and we ourselves do not rule anything). Eternal Life, totally PROVIDED FOR US by God; coming to us in our experience; causing us to grow (attended by growing pains). Our rule and God's rule cannot coexist, and only HIS can exist in His Kingdom

Jesus, _for the joy that was to be His, endured the cross and despised the shame_ (Hebrews 12:2, KJV), all to make possible our Life . . . OUR LIFE . . . HE knew what He was going through, and why, and He went through it FOR US!

At any given point, WE will not know but we CAN trust Him to bring us through our cross; enable us to despise OUR shame; to go through OUR "growing pains" INTO.OUR. ETERNAL.LIFE

He Is Here !!!

At a recent gathering, one brother spoke that we should NOT be deceived as to the reality of the presence of God IN OUR EVERY CIRCUMSTANCE. Another brother spoke of the need to be sure to acknowledge His presence in the very trying, painful, and un-understandable things that come our way.

As I have considered these things, I have come to believe that when the DIFFICULT times come our way, those are the times when we get to see what we really believe about the nature of God. Do we REALLY believe He is perfect love? Do we REALLY believe He loves US as an individual? Do we REALLY BELIEVE He is powerful enough to take care of OUR particular issue? Is it REALLY true that if I ask, I will receive? And is it REALLY true that all of His good stuff is FREELY GIVEN, and not dependent on whether or not I deserve it?; <u>that it is ALL a matter of His GRACE?</u> These things, as well as some others, are things we must consider for ourselves IN OUR DIFFICULT TIMES. Deciding these matters is usually NOT EASY, but if we would truly know Him, we need to press forward to Truth . . . the truth of these matters . . . as they pertain and apply to us personally.

However, as difficult as it is to see God as He Truly is in the midst of our trying times, it is much more tricky to see Him as He Truly is with relation to us when the circumstances are NOT difficult; when life is good; when we are NOT in a struggle with anything. At those times it is so easy for us to be content with ourselves; to fail to recognize in our hearts our continual need for HIM; the fact of our continuous dependence on HIM at all times . . . in these "good" times, equally as much as in our "bad" times.

So, the reality of our beliefs about Him and His nature are tested when things are tough, but the reality of our beliefs about our need of and our dependence on Him in ALL situations is not tested when things are smooth and easy

He wants us to pass both these tests, and find His Life.

If-Then

<u>53.- All that God does, He does out of and</u>
<u>because of HIMSELF: NOT BECAUSE OF</u>
<u>something I do. (one of my "pearls")</u>

So a sister asks,"what about the if-then scriptures ?"

Great question, I'D say: made me actually THINK about it, and
while I was thinking, this is what I thunk:

First of all, there ARE a large number of those "if-then"
scriptures, starting maybe with the Lord speaking to <u>Cain</u> before
he killed his brother <u>Abel</u>, saying <u>"IF you do well (THEN) you</u>
<u>shall be accepted, and IF you do not do well (THEN) sin crouches</u>
<u>at the door;</u> then through Moses, recorded in <u>Deuteronomy 28</u>
regarding both the blessings and the curses (if-then), and so on,
then on through Jesus saying <u>"IF any man will come after me</u>
<u>(THEN) let him deny himself and take up his cross and follow me"</u>;
and <u>"If any man can believe (If THOU canst believe) (THEN)</u>
<u>NOTHING shall be impossible"</u>. <u>"Ask and you shall receive" (IF</u>
<u>you ask, THEN you will receive)</u>, on to I John, <u>"IF a man says he</u>
<u>loves God, but hates his brother (THEN) THAT man is a liar"</u>. <u>"IF</u>
<u>any man be in Christ (THEN) he is a new creature"</u>, etc.

So I'm thinking that this is how things look from the human
side of things: and we have a need pretty regularly to hear what
will happen if we do such-and-such . . . or if we DON"T do

"xyz" . . . these kinds of statements, as well as direct instructions are needful to us as humans to help channel us to the Lord.

These words are true and necessary: they instruct us as to how things are; how God is; how HE has designed stuff to WORK; what LIFE looks like, etc. They are ALL, however, sourced in God. He knows everything about everything before anything came to be, and He desires to communicate to us, His creation, how things ARE. Yet the truths at the base of His Words of instruction (including the "if-thens") . . . those truths exist whether or not any person heard them.

So since we all started out separated from Him, and since His desire is to draw us separated creatures <u>TO</u> Him, He needed to find a way to show us how to return. (His forgiveness extended toward us through the death of His Son being the primary demonstration, but His directions, including the "if-then"s are all in place to help us understand what we need to understand in order to find and experience that Life which we had lost.)

He, Who sees everything at all times, can very easily know where any step we take; any action; even any thought we may have will take us: NOT because He is "writing the terms of the contract", so to speak, but because HE KNOWS, and because He knows, He desires to show us the specifics we need.

This is quite similar to what a doctor might very well tell us, such as "if you keep on eating sugary food, you will most likely gain a lot of weight which will be harmful to your body and your health, and most likely you will get diabetes, also very harmful to you", or "if you keep thinking negative thoughts, it will hurt your physical health", or "if you think positive thoughts, your whole life will improve". Of course these statements are based on what that doctor has learned, and generally they are true, and we ought generally to give heed. With God, however, His knowledge is absolute and is specific to us each individually, so when He tells us basically to quit worrying about anything but instead bring all our concerns to Him, asking (even begging) for what we need, thankfully, telling Him all our requests, and His Peace will guard our hearts, He gives us this instruction BECAUSE THAT IS HOW THINGS ARE and He desires through this instruction to draw us close to Him, which is where we belong. IF we will follow those instructions, THEN WE WILL have His peace: NOT because that is His rule and we gotta "toe the line", so to speak, but BECAUSE THAT IS HOW THESE THINGS WORK.

So . . . when we human creatures behold His instructions (including His "if-then"s), it is wise for us to give heed: not because He's got a bunch of rules we hafta follow just because He's God, but because He is wanting to show us how things ARE . . . and how they have been since long before we existed.

So the "if-thens" are true and needful for us humans, yet with God, _"FROM Him and THROUGH Him and TO Him are ALL things"_: to HIM be the glory!

Signs

So I'm driving along, minding my own business, when all of a sudden, out of the blue with no warning whatsoever, a sign just appears off to the right side of the road: one of them yellow rhomboidal signs, you know, like a square sign tipped on an angle so one corner points straight up, and the other corners point . . . well you know . . . anyway, on that sign is an arrow that curves quite sharply to the left and underneath the arrow is written "25 MPH" . . . what the??? WHO put that sign there? Who do they think they are? Do they think by putting their old sign there that I will slow down to 25 MPH? Really! Who are THEY to try to control me? The VERY idea!!! Well I'll show them! Not only will I not slow down to 25 MPH, I'm gonna step on it and go even faster!

Well, after the dumb tow truck FINALLY gets there and pulls me out of the ditch (what a STUPID place to put a ditch), I continue on my trip to see my cousin out in Wisconsin. After a few more miles, I see aNOTHER of them tipped-square signs off to the right side of the road, and on it is what looks like a "T", like they're expecting me to stop and turn either right or left in only fifty feet. Is this the same guy who put up that other sign, or just one of his relatives? Well I'm not turning !!!!!

So after another tow truck comes along and pulls me out of the living room (why would anybody build a house in a place like that? Just plain STUPID is what I'd say)! (though it WAS pretty funny, seeing the looks on the faces of the family at their dining room table!)

Anyhow, the front of my nice car is really crunched up now so I can't drive at all, and the tow truck has to take me to a nearby (only thirty-seven miles away) auto body place, and after a wait of eighteen days (why can't they fix my car when I NEED them to?) I finally get on the road again, but by then my cousin doesn't have any more time off, (what's wrong with that place he works, anyway?) so there's no sense going on to Wisconsin, and they're telling me I've gotta pay to have that hole in the wall patched. Spoiled the whole trip . . . just because of them stupid signs . . .

What? What's that? You think I'm silly? Stupid? You say those signs were put there to HELP me? To give me a SAFE trip? Not just to tell me how to run my life? Really? . . . hmmmmm . . . well, OK . . . I suppose you're right.

So I'm wondering, what about the signs God puts up? You know: "Do This" . . . "Do That" . . . "Don't Do This" . . . "Don't Do That" . . . "Believe This" . . . etc. Signs like that . . . God is very old, you know (or so they say). Probably Senile, don't you think? Definitely not Educated or Sophisticated or Progressive or Enlightened like WE are, if He even EXISTS. What possible good are THOSE signs?

But what if He's <u>NOT</u> outdated, and His signs <u>ARE</u> there for my good ?

Lust

In <u>Peters' second "epistle"</u>, he writes (<u>chapter 1:verses 3 & 4</u>) that <u>God, by His power and because of His excellence and glory, has given us promises: Very great and precious promises, so that we may partake of and share in His Divine Nature and so that we can escape the corruption that is in the world, caused by human desire (caused by lust)</u>. LUST (the KJV word) . . . this lust brought about ALL the corruption that is in the world today.

I'm thinking that nobody has a problem agreeing that there is a lot of corruption in todays' world: it seems like no matter where we look, there it is, and I think that in general most of us have some idea about what causes it: somebody (or a bunch of somebodies) did something they shouldn't have done, and some other somebodies got hurt (or worse). I think that's the kind of thing <u>Peter</u> wrote about, so I thought I'd look into this "lust" thing a bit.

If anyone would like a list of the scriptures used for this writing, "ask, and you shall receive". I am not planning on using many in the writing itself. I have used Vines' Expository Dictionary quite a bit, in addition to the scripture: check it out if you like.

So, we got a problem: CORRUPTION . . . and as <u>Peter</u> says, it's here by means of lust. That word, right there in the Bible! So now, all we gotta figger out is, what IS this "lust" thing?

When most of us hear that word, we think about warped; twisted; unreasonable; over-powering sexual desire, and certainly very few would argue that there IS a lot of corruption in this world as a product of this kind of sexual desire . . . BUT . . . is this what <u>Peter</u> is talking about ? Sorry, but NO. That's only a very tiny part of it. Well, WHAT, then ?

I think one thing that oughtta be mentioned is that "lust" (in and of itself) is not necessarily a bad thing. Sometimes, in fact, it is a very GOOD thing. Ask if you want some scripture, but as a couple of examples, we are encouraged to strongly desire spiritual gifts; and love (God-love, or agape love). Enough to say that it is not BAD to desire or to want many things. Similar words that describe this are human desire; pleasure; passion; longing after, etc. The point here is that this "lust" thing is a normal part of our human life. Everybody wants stuff of some sort, and some of that stuff we want with a very strong, nearly overpowering desire . . . it is . . . simply part of how we (all) are: we ALL want things!

Having said that, it is important (as I see it) to make the distinction between THIS understanding of "lust" and that spoken of by <u>Peter</u> when he speaks of the corruption that is in the world . . . through "lust" . . . to be much more blunt, darling, it is YOUR strong desires (and that of all the rest of us) that has brought corruption into this world. <u>James chapter 4</u> lists something of how this works: you want stuff and don't have it, so you do all kinds of things: lying, cheating, stealing, fighting, killing, etc. Think how you felt when you didn't get something you rilly, rilly, rilly wanted . . . what did you do? (or maybe you didn't actually DO, but thought of doing). Can ya see it? THIS is the kind of thing that <u>Peter</u> wrote about (and <u>James</u>) . . . and we are ALL guilty of it . . . don't you agree?

BUT . . . it is still not wrong to desire stuff! We have been told by <u>Jesus</u> to ask; to seek; and to knock. We are told to cast all our cares on Him; to let our requests be known to God; to trust in the Lord with all our heart; not to depend on our own understanding; to acknowledge God . . . IN . . . ALL . . . our circumstances, etc. All these instructions carry a related promise (like <u>Peter</u> was writing about) to help us escape the corruption!

One account has helped clarify all this for me: it is the account of <u>Jesus</u> in the garden of Gethsemane: exceedingly sorrowful; near death; sweating, like great drops of blood. Have you ever experienced that kind of thing? No, and neither have I, but THAT was a HUGE, screaming desire, wouldn't you agree?

(From Matthew 26, AMP): *"He began to show grief and distress of mind, and was deeply depressed. Then He said to them, my soul is very sad, and deeply grieved so that I am almost dying of sorrow . . . and . . going a little further, He threw Himself on the ground on His face and prayed, saying, My Father, if it is possible, let this cup pass away from me; nevertheless, not what I will (what I desire), but as You will and desire"* (and from <u>Luke 22:41-44, AMP</u>) . . . *"He withdrew from them about a stone's throw and knelt down and prayed, saying, Father, if you are willing, remove this cup from Me; yet not My will but [always] Yours be done . . . and there appeared to Him and angel from Heaven, strengthening Him in spirit. And being in an agony of mind, He prayed all the more earnestly and intently, and His sweat became like great clots of blood dropping down upon the ground."*

I would never try to deny that you have experienced extreme pain, with accompanying extreme desire, and I have no desire to minimize that at all: and the desires that most of us have do not approach that level, though it may certainly at times be most intense, as is the case in my own experience. So I want to be sure to say that it is totally normal for us to have desires; some of them extreme. . . . normal . . . and usually understandable, certainly most of the time. So we all have these desires; perfectly normal and natural for us humans: yet it is these desires that bring corruption into our world. What are we to do?

For those of us who belong to the Lord, there is one answer (in addition to what is in four paragraphs back: it is the answer <u>Jesus</u> showed us in the garden, and it is this ONE thing that determines whether or not OUR desires will be contributing to the corruption in the world. <u>Jesus</u> expressed it in these words: *"<u>Nevertheless, NOT what I will (what I desire), BUT AS YOU WILL AND DESIRE</u>"*

This is the ONE thing we can do to ensure that our desires will not add to this worlds' corruption, and it is the ONE thing that points to what makes "lust" a bad thing . . . it is . . . ready for it? "Lust" . . . the bad kind . . . is <u>UNSUBMITTED DESIRE</u>. In the same sentence, I think it is best to remind ourselves that Jesus has forgiven ALL that! It still brings corruption, and we oughtta give very serious heed. But yet, for all those who belong to Him, even when we DON'T submit our desires, BECAUSE OF JESUS, WE ARE FORGIVEN! AMAZING!

I am hoping in this writing to make three (at least) things as clear as I can:

1. - (for those of us who truly belong to the Lord) We have been absolutely and totally forgiven because Jesus died on our behalf, and in our place: for us, there are NO exceptions! ALL has been forgiven . . . totally . . . this includes every instance where we have followed our own desires by our own means.

2. - The fact that we have been totally forgiven does not alter the truth that following our own desires (unsubmitted) always leads to corruption (is contrary to what the Lord has purposed for us and for the world).

3. - Presenting our desires to the Lord and waiting for His response; then, acting in accordance with His response (I have listed some of the "how-to's" of that, above,) is the ONLY way for us to avoid spreading corruption in the world, because we have then put our will and wishes UNDER Gods' will and wishes, and submitted to HIS way in our lives. We have then passed on LIFE rather than corruption!

This is a choice we are required to make: follow our own desires, and create corruption . . . or . . . submit our own desires to Him and agree with HIM, and participate in spreading Life.

Learning to be Content

As some of you know, I have recently written on the matter of lust: to summarize very briefly, there is a lot of corruption in this world, and it has gotten here through lust; through strong personal desires which have not been submitted to God . . . so . . . what can we look to that will help us deal with those desires? To summarize, once again, the basic tool we have is to submit whatever those desires are to God, and be communicating with Him on-goingly about 'em, and asking Him for the thing(s) we are wanting; and, of course, listening to whatever He might be saying to us. This much we have already written (refer back to the "Lust" writing for more detail if you'd like, but in addition to that, we have the opportunity to (as our elder brother said to the Philippian church) "Learn to be content IN EVERY SITUATION" . . . I hope to explore this learning thing somewhat in this writing.

Let me quote from the Amplified version of the Bible from _Philippians 4:11-13:_"_I have learned how to become content (satisfied to the point where I am not disturbed or disquieted) in whatever state I am, for I know how to be abased and live humbly in (tough) circumstances, and I know how to enjoy plenty and live in abundance. I have learned in any and all circumstances the secret of facing every situation, whether well-fed or going hungry, having a sufficiency and enough to spare or going without and being in want. I have strength for all things_ *in Christ Who empowers me (I am ready for anything and equal to anything through Him Who infuses inner strength into me: I am self-sufficient IN CHRISTS' SUFFICIENCY).*

Most of us are more familiar with "I can do all things through Christ Who strengthens me" (which has been grossly lifted from its context and therefore taken to mean something never intended by brother Paul): so let's get to what he WAS saying, OK?

One of the first things that caught my attention is that he HAD LEARNED: this was not something that "came naturally" to him as a man; he LEARNED it. OK, but HOW did he learn it"?, I'm wondering. It seems to me that he learned it by going THROUGH both the wonderful stuff AND the terrible stuff. He told the Corinthian bunch of believers that he had been whipped by the Jews five times; beaten with rods three times; stoned once (this is not something drug-related); shipwrecked three times; a day and a night "floating/swimming in the sea; frequent journeys; perils in the water; perils from robbers; from his own countrymen; from the heathen; in the city; in the wilderness; weariness; painfulness; hunger; thirst; frequent fasting; cold; nakedness: and then the burden of caring for the churches! How's THAT for a list? I know that all of us have gone through (might even now be going through) very hard stuff. I have (and still presently am). anybody got a list that compares with that of brother Paul? Not me.

Quite a few of us, in those sorts of circumstances, tend to get angry; bitter; resistive; etc. But brother Paul learned to be content . . . I'm supposing that all of us, brother Paul included, do not have any problem being content when all the good stuff's happening, but when we're going through the tough stuff? Content? Prolly not, I'm guessing, at least not at first. We gotta LEARN it, just like brother Paul had to learn it . . . but HOW?

I think what I'm learning is that it's what's going on inside us (the Life of God IN us) that is the key. Saying it another way, it is not possible for us to get content with the hard stuff going on except by the power of HIS LIFE. It is the nature of HIS Life to be content at all times . . . so I'm thinking that the main thing here is that we need to "learn" to allow His Life to overcome our natural reactions.

Foundational to all this is that we come to the solid conviction of a couple of things: First, that God actually really LOVES us: not like our human definition of love, but the kind of love that wants the very best for all of us. Then, that He is unlimited in His power . . . his ability to do WHATEVER He chooses. So I think we have to let Him convince us of these two basic things if we are to learn to be content. It means basically that NOTHING touches our life (either wonderful or excruciatingly painful) except He wills it or at least allows it, if not causes it: for our good (and of course for His ultimate glory). The fact that we cannot understand it, or do not like it, does not change these basic truths.

OK well I'm gonna get personal and blunt with ya here: when the tough stuff arrives on your doorstep, what's the first thing you're gonna do? Get mad? Sulk? Throw a pity-party? Invite a bunch of friends over so they will know how bad things are? rebuke the devil? What? Cry? . . . pray for healing? . . . I think there are certainly times, when things hurt, to cry: maybe even get real' angry; and certainly there are times we oughtta rebuke the devil, but the FIRST thing really needs to be ACCEPTING it (because, as we have said or more specifically as HE has said) He Who is perfect Love (He Who loves us each personally) has either called it to be or allowed it to be, toward a wonderful purpose. We ACCEPT it: (as Hannah Hurnard says it, it is "acceptance with Joy". It IS the next step in our developing new Life, which is why it is vital to first of all accept it: THEN we go to HIM about it and find out what's next . . . HE knows . . . and of course WE never do know, really.

I think these are all things we need to LEARN, and because of His Life inside us, we WILL learn! And because of that Life, we will be content: that is His nature, and for those of us who are His, it becomes OUR nature. We shall learn, and we shall become . . . CONTENT! . . . and . . . in this place of contentment we will not have unsubmitted strong desires, because in the process of becoming content, we will have submitted all our desires to Him Who cares about every aspect of our lives!

Priorities

We need to get our priorities in order, we are told . . . but what does that mean? What does it look like? . . . OK . . . we gotta make a list: a list of everything in our lives . . . let's see . . . there's God, of course, and everybody knows He's gotta be FIRST! Then there's my spouse, if I have one and my job and my ministry (EVERY Christian's gotta have one of those, ya know. Then there's my family, (including each of my children)and my relaxation time and my hobbies and the church. What did I miss?

So now I gotta organize these, with the most important at the top, and the least important at the bottom: oughtta be easy, right? So we've heard "JESUS first, OTHERS second, and YOU last: J-O-Y, the recipe for joy, right? So I know for sure that God is first and I am last. Got that, but how to organize the "others"? Well, if I have a spouse I suppose they would be a close second to God, right? OK, got that. I suppose my kids might be next in importance, right? Then maybe my "ministry"?, then prolly other "church" activities. Maybe next would be my job: or should these last two be reversed? Then there's the "me" stuff (ya know, my hobby, relaxation time, etc.): so here it is:

1. - God
2. - Spouse

3. - Children (equal time for all five of 'em, (cuz they're all equal, and should have equal attention, as you know)
4. - Ministry
5. - Church activities
6. - Job
7. - Me

PERFECT!!!!!!!!: Seven items!!! The number of perfection! Now let's figure out how it will all work . . . let's see . . . my job requires eight hours at work, plus a half hour travel each way . . . that's nine hours out of my twenty-four, but if God is more important than my job (and who could argue with that?), then I need to give Him more time than that so let's give Him ten hours each day. Well now nineteen hours of each day are taken care of, which leaves me with five hours for my spouse, my children, (all five of 'em), my ministry, my church activities, and my "me" time . . . and I didn't even THINK about sleep . . . oh me: I believe I am in trouble! Of course I only work 5 days a week: not on the weekend, so those extra two days of my weekend could be added to my five hours, now giving me fifty-three hours for my spouse, my children (all 5 of 'em), my ministry, my church activities, and my ""me" time (and please, some sleep)! But everybody knows we humans need about 8 hours of sleep each of the seven nights, totaling 56 hours a week for sleep . . . but I only have fifty-three hours, leaving me short three hours, but now I have NO time for my spouse, my children (all five of 'em), my ministry, my church activities, and my "me" time . I am in deep trouble here guys: HELP!!!!!!!

But OK: suppose I HAVE figured a way to do this: on any given day, how do I know I have devoted adequate time to each responsibility? When have I given child #3 enough attention so I don't need to give any more to #3? What if she falls down and scrapes her knee? or cuts her finger? or can't seem to get to sleep? Must she wait for tomorrow for her allotted time/attention slot? If not, whom may I rob of THEIR slot (from my list), and how do I make it up to that one? What if my wife is having a particularly difficult time today? (or is she not allowed to have that kind of day?) Is child #3 not allowed to fall down or cut her finger or have trouble getting to sleep? I am thinking right now that I really need to abandon this whole priority thing . . . but what then? How can I ever run my life right?

Could it be that I am not SUPPOSED to run the whole show? I have heard that God thinks He is capable of running . . . well . . . EVERYTHING, so does that include what goes on between me and Him? Me and my spouse? Me and all five of my children? My ministry, and all my church activities? Me and my job? Me and my "me-time"? Can He REALLY DO all that???

What if all "my" stuff and responsibilities are not really MINE? What if they are HIS, and HE can show me whatever I need to be doing to do my part in taking care of whatever He has entrusted to me to steward? Can He really DO that? Will He do that? Can I trust Him?

HE said, "the steps of a good man are ordered by the Lord" . . . steps: like, EVERY step? Ordered . . . Ordered? He ORDERS them? HE said that the heart of a man devises his way, BUT THE LORD ORDERS HIS STEPS . . . there we go again . . . then HE says I'm to TRUST HIM with ALL (all???) my heart; to acknowledge HIM in all MY ways and then HE will direct my paths. So He's gonna ORDER my steps AND DIRECT my paths? ORDER . . . AND DIRECT . . which leaves me to do . . . exactly WHAT? . . . whatever HE orders and directs, I suppose.

HE also said that is we would seek FIRST His Kingdom

and His Righteousness, that He would take care of other stuff we need: seek FIRST What does THAT mean? First thing in the morning, and then I'm free to do whatever other things I really want to do, or feel I MUST do?

But He doesn't want to be first on any list of things no matter how good those things might be: not first, that way: He wants to be first in the sense of being CENTRAL IN ALL OUR THINGS, so that HE will be free to ORDER AND DIRECT "my" stuff according to His plan. I think I will like this, if I will DO it. MUCH less burden on MY back: much less stress . . . rest . . . HE knows THE Priority in any given moment of my life so I can relax in that.

So now, He will be the center, ordering and directing (calling the shots, so to speak) my relationship with Him; with my spouse; with each of my five children; my ministry and other church activities; my job; and my "me-time", all of which are no longer "mine", but His. HIM at the center, just like it's SUPPOSED to be. Well OK!

James 4:3

*"You ask and do not receive,
because you ask with wrong motives, so that you
may spend it on your lusts"* (my paraphrase).

God is good enough and wise enough to sometimes answer our prayers with a firm "NO."

If HE were to give us what we ask when our motives are wrong, then HE would be feeding some ungodly lust that would only grow and become more demanding and destructive over time, ultimately releasing death into our lives in multiple ways. Thankfully God does NOT feed our lusts: even when we pray.

Sometimes we are blind to our own lusts and deceitful motivations, but God is NEVER deceived. He sees right into the core of our beings and knows exactly what is motivating us in every moment of our lives including our prayer-lives.

Proverbs 16:2, KJV states, *"All the ways of a man are clean in his own sight, But the LORD weighs the motives."* God is checking our motivations. And 1 Corinthians 4:5, KJV tells us that *"…the Lord … will both bring to light the things hidden in the darkness and disclose the motives of men's hearts…"*

Greed could motivate me to pray that I will get another raise in pay [*which according to me I richly deserve*], or I that should certainly win the Lottery. While my greed might be obvious to others it may not be at all that clear to me. Thankfully, because

God is love, He just may give me a "NO" so that He does not feed my lust for wealth or possessions. He IS a good God!

Of course when I ask for healing, I might simply want to feel better. That is not necessarily a bad thing and it is certainly understandable, unless, of course, I desire to use my new-found health to chase my own dreams rather than live pursuing HIS purposes. Would it be "good" then for HIM to deny my request? Or, would it be "good" to heal me no matter what I purpose to do with my remaining life?

It is certain that God knows far better than I what would be 'good' for me and what would be destructive for me. Not only does He know but because He is both loving and good He must act accordingly.

Then, there is this question: What is motivating me to pray for a healing or a miracle for you? Surely, I could be motivated by the love and compassion of God . . . or . . . I could want to look good and be recognized as a "mighty man of God" or I could be operating with a mixed bag of both 'compassion' and 'personal agenda. God might need to say, "NO" because of my lusts or prideful religious agenda. Or He might say, "YES" out of compassion for you, and at the same time take steps to deal with my wrong motivations.

I am convinced that God would LOVE to give us ALL KINDS OF GOOD THINGS. The problem is never that God is unable or unwilling. He, who is love, always considers the long-term results of His giving: He maintains an eternal focus even when we do not. His work is to prepare us *internally* in order to release His goodness *externally* to us and through us so that HE can reward us *eternally*.

In Matthew 7:7-11, KJV Jesus also encouraged us to pray saying, *"Ask, and it will be given to you; seek, and you will find; knock, and it will be opened to you.* [8] *"For everyone who asks receives, and he who seeks finds, and to him who knocks it will be opened. [9] "Or what man is there among you who, when his son asks for a loaf, will give him a stone? [10] "Or if he asks for a fish, he will not give him a snake, will he? [11] "If you then, being evil, know how to give good gifts to your children, how much more will your Father who is in heaven give what is good to those who ask Him!"*

Notice that here again is this very critical principal that *"your Father who is in heaven [will] give what is good to those who ask Him!"* Certainly while an earthly father wants to give good things to his children, he, even then must often answer with a firm "NO!" [*even if the child throws a temper-tantrum*]. But no matter how hard we try, we earthly parents do not parent perfectly, resulting in various degrees of immaturity, pain, destruction, and even death to our offspring. God is perfect in His parenting and that perfection causes Him to appear less than perfect or even loving in the eyes of His kids because of their [our] immaturity and childish [fleshly] agendas.

Today as you pray, ask Him for a heart that is made pure by His love and presence. May it be that your prayers flow out a heart that is so tuned to His that they will bring abundant life and blessing to you and those around you and great joy to the heart of the Father.

> *"Now all glory to God, who is able, through His mighty power at work within us, to accomplish infinitely more than we might ask or think."*
> Ephesians 3:20, AMP

King of kings . . . Lord of lords

Many times in the scripture God is referred to as the King of kings and the Lord of lords, but what exactly does that mean? I suppose I don't know EXACTLY what it means, but a few thoughts have crossed my mind during these times when some campaigns for this or that election are going on. So since I know you're dying to hear (in a figure of speech) what I might be thinking about this, I'm gonna letcha know some of them thoughts:

First of all, what IS a king? The sense of what I've read says that a king is an individual with awesome power and responsibility, and when speaking of God as King, we see a picture of His invisible but real rule over the course of human events (this from Vines' definition)

But we're talking here about Him being the King . . . of kings . . . or we might say OVER kings. WHAT other kings, we might well ask? Are there any kings over which He is NOT ruler? What about governors? Mayors? Prime Ministers? And more to the point of THIS writing, what about Presidents? Does He rule over Presidents?

God seems to think He is over ALL them guys !

Romans 13:1 tells us there is NO authority except from God, and those which exist are established by God, and Psalms103:19 tells us that the Lord has established His throne. His sovereignty rules over ALL!

Then to <u>Colossians 1:16, KJV</u>, where we are told that *"<u>By Him ALL things were created, in the heavens and on the earth, visible and invisible, whether THRONES or DOMINIONS or RULERS or AUTHORITIES: ALL things have been created through Him and FOR HIM."</u>*

I Chronicles 29:12, KJV: *"<u>Both riches and honor come of YOU, and You reign over ALL; and in your hand is power and might; and it is in Your hand to make great and to give strength unto ALL."</u>*

Then <u>Psalms 47:2, KJV</u> *"<u>The Lord Most High is terrible; He is a Great King over ALL THE EARTH."</u>*

Back to <u>Romans 11:36, KJV</u> *"<u>FROM Him and THROUGH Him and TO Him are ALL things"</u>*

And <u>Psalms 75:6 & 7, KJV</u> *"<u>not from the east nor from the west comes exaltation; but God is the judge." HE PUTS DOWN ONE AND EXALTS ANOTHER."</u>*

And even more specifically, <u>Daniel 2:20 & 21, KJV</u> tells us, *"<u>blessed be the Name of God forever and ever; for wisdom and might are His: He changes the times and the seasons: He REMOVES KINGS, AND SETS UP KINGS"</u>*

Then after He is done all this "removing . . . and setting up . . . and exalting", then He says in <u>Proverbs 21:1, KJV</u> *"<u>The kings' heart is as channels of water in the hand of the Lord; He turns it wherever He wishes."</u>*

So why are you telling me all this stuff? you may ask . . . ok, I'll TELL ya . . . I've been talking with and listening to and reading about many (if not most) of those in my circle of existence, who are very emotionally entangled with the stuff that one or another of the present political candidates is saying; with what this one or that one supposedly did; with the half-truth (lies) being spoken about this man or that one; with the medias' slant on all of it; with the trampling of honor; with the "un-Christian" beliefs and behaviors of this candidate or that one (and therefore engaging in severe judgements against this or that one); etc.

Can this type of behavior be justified by any one of us who claim to be following after Christ (living His Life)? I'm thinking many think it is perfectly good, maybe even Godly Personally, I think not! Is HE all upset about any of this? I doubt it, and if He is not, why ought WE get all drawn into it all? Why can we not simply go about exercising our part in this democratic process, without all this angst?

Contrary to what many believe, the democratic system of governance is NOT the best (even if the democratic system had not been mangled and warped [though it has been] so it is not even a true democracy). The BEST form of governance is God Himself (but we humans have rejected that for a very long time): so we are left in this country with a broken democratic system. Why not, in quietness and peace of heart, work within that system: doing whatever research, etc. that we may, and when it is time simply cast our ballot the best way we can: but for those of us who claim to believe in the Lord, it is MY thought that underneath all that, foundational to all of that, is the reality that God (in OUR case primarily working through and with our "democratic" system), that it will be God Who determines who our next president will be.

So we humans have tried to basically kick Him off His throne and taken it upon ourselves to govern ourselves, developing our own systems so WE can decide things like who our next president will be But for some reason HE did not fall off His throne: He lets us play our power games, and actually BY THOSE GAMES, HE . . . tears down and sets up . . . I said HE does that. Personally, I think THIS should guide us as we get set up to make OUR vote known.

He says He sets up (presidents): George W. Bush? He set HIM up? Or Barack Obama? He set HIM up? Whaddaya think? Did THEY slip "under His radar", so to speak? If He actually DID set those men up, what is He up to? WHY, for goodness sake, would He choose THOSE guys?

But now, can WE stop getting all tangled up in what the world is trying to throw at us? Could we ask HIM about the voting thing? Could we, ya know, stay in peace, simply doing the best we know (or think we know)? Personally, that is how I am aimed: how 'bout YOU?

The Word of God

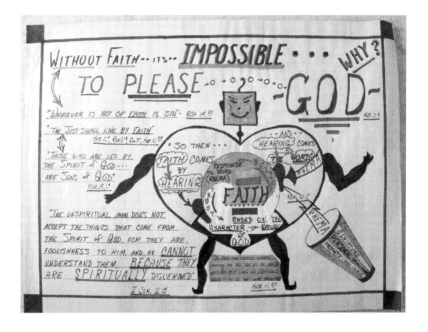

I was looking through my concordance the other day, checking to see what I could find about how the phrase "the Word of God" is used in the Bible. The first thing I "discovered" is that there are about thirty zillion (more or less) references to that phrase in the Bible: WOW ! What an adventure in writing THAT would be! thirty zillion (more or less) references, plus comments on each one! That would be . . . well . . . a really

L…O…N…G writing: ya know, I am really . . . just not quite prepared for that, so I ditched the idea. (say thank you)

So the second thing I noticed as I was scanning through this list is that whenever that phrase appeared ("the Word of God", or "the Word of the Lord") it NEVER referred to the Bible. Now don't be getting upset here: I LOVE the Bible! I study it and meditate on it and I have memorized quite a bit of it. It is Scripture, and as Peter writes (<u>II Peter 2:20 & 21</u>), it is NOT in any way a human document: it is, rather, the result of holy men of God being moved (spoken to) by Holy Spirit, and spoke and wrote what they were hearing . . . Timothy writes (<u>II Timothy 3:15-17</u>) that *<u>the sacred writings (Torah: the Scripture) are given by inspiration of God (God-breathed), and it is valuable for instruction; for reproof and conviction of sin; for correction of error and discipline in obedience; for training in holy living; for conformity to God's will in thought, purpose, and action; for making us complete and mature and for making us well-fitted and thoroughly equipped for every good work.</u>* WOW ! . . . now THAT is quite a mouthful!

So the value of scripture is not to be questioned: HOWEVER, it is NOT the <u>ONLY</u> Word of God spoken of in the scriptures. In this writing I am hoping to show (by using the scriptures) (I'll simply say, "the Bible" from now on) that His Word comes to us in possibly un-numberable (is that a word?) ways, through so many different channels.

To kick off our thinking, let's consider the last verse of the book of John (<u>John 21:25</u>). John (one of those "holy men of God") spoke as moved by God, and said that Jesus did so much more than he had been able to record. So much more, in fact, that if it COULD HAVE BEEN recorded, the whole world wouldn't be big enough to contain all the books, and that was talking about the stuff He DID! And what about the Words He SPOKE? They would be a lot more, wouldn't ya say? So I think it wouldn't be too much of a stretch to think that God has spoken MUCH more than what's recorded in the pages of the Bible . . . would it?

OK . . . so . . . as we continue thinking about this, let's also keep in mind (as foundational to our thoughts) this other Word of God given to Malachi (<u>Malachi 3:6, KJV</u>) which says "*<u>I am the Lord, and I DO NOT CHANGE</u>*" . . . pretty much repeated in the book of Hebrews (<u>Hebrews 13:8, KJV</u>), referring to Jesus, "*<u>the same, yesterday; today; forever.</u>*"

So now, let's take a peek at a few specifics FROM SCRIPTURE, OK? First of all, let's think about the number of references in the Bible where we can read such things as "<u>The Lord said to</u>" Moses, or Abraham, or Joshua, or Job: on and on) *you can check this out for yourself by reading for yourself through,* *for example,* <u>*Exodus*</u> *or* <u>*Leviticus*</u> *or* <u>*Job*</u>: or "<u>the Word of the Lord came to</u>" <u>Ezekiel</u>, or <u>Daniel</u>, or <u>Hosea</u>, or <u>Joel</u>, or <u>Isaiah</u>, or <u>Jeremiah,</u> etc. The Lord had several conversations with <u>Baalam</u> (*at least one time through the mouth of his donkey*).

Let's slow down now, and think about a few of those occasions: <u>Moses</u>, at the burning bush, talking with God . . . talking with God? . . . That's what it SAYS! (<u>Exodus 3 & 4</u>) Was somebody hunkered down behind the bush, reading the Torah or Ephesians to him? Seems doubtful to me: You? How about <u>Adam & Eve</u> in the garden? Or <u>Moses</u>, later on, getting instruction from the Lord about things to pass on to the Israelites? (<u>Exodus 19, 20, 21 etc. plus most of the book of Leviticus</u>): Who was reading the Bible to him then? (now don't be forgetting: God never changes!) How about <u>Jonah</u>, when God told him to go to Ninevah (<u>Jonah 1:1</u>) or later, after he went through his big fish thing (after God told the fish to spit him out) . . . wait . . . wait . . . God . . . spoke to a FISH??? (if that's not enough, check out <u>JOB 12:8&9</u>: <u>THE FISH WILL DECLARE IT.</u> Well it DOES say that, doesn't it?

(Jonah 2:10). And later, after he had preached in Ninevah and God didn't destroy those awful sinners and Jonah was mad at God, and he and God had a conversation: Bible ??? I'm thinking not. You ???

Then of course there is the Lord speaking to His prophets: you know, Isaiah, Jeremiah, Ezekiel, Daniel, Hosea, Joel, Amos, Obadiah, Micah, Nahum, Habakkuk, Zephaniah, Haggai, Zechariah, and Malachi. Many times the Bible says God told them stuff through visions, and other time He just told 'em . . . Bible? . . . Nope, He did it Himself. And He said He's the same yesterday, today, and forever, remember? And sometimes He spoke to His people through angels, and sometimes through dreams (think about Mary and Joseph (early Mathew and Luke). Bible? Again, nope: the Bible tells US about it, but it was not the Bible that spoke to Joseph or to Mary, was it?

Then, how about Saul of Tarsus: persecutor of the church, later on becoming an apostle and writer of a lot of the New Testament (Acts 9 plus) Did the Bible knock him off his donkey? Most likely not, I'm thinking. How about Cornelius (and Peter) (Acts 10)? . . . and how about the apostle John on the Isle of Patmos (think, the book of the Revelation)?

In Psalm 19:1-4, the Scripture declares that all the stuff of creation proclaims the Glory of God, echoed by Paul in Romans 1:20. The Word of God is coming to us through all of creation !

How about in the first verses of the gospel of John: "in the beginning was" . . . WHAT? . . . What was in the beginning? The Word: In the beginning was THE WORD, Who was WITH God and who WAS God. (I think it's worth some meditation . . . the thing about God's Word BEING GOD). Of course when we hear the word "Word", we don't tend to think of it that way, do we ? Nope . . . THIS "Word" is a "He"!

THE ONE Who created everything that has been created! THE WORD does all that, and not only that, but THE WORD of God (Hebrews 11:3 plus) tells us, that HE (THE WORD) framed everything, and presently upholds it and sustains it.

A little sorta "side-trip" here: Faith . . . pretty important for us Christians, wouldn't you say? Romans 10:17 tells us that faith comes by hearing: AND HEARING COMES BY THE WORD, Or, we gotta HEAR something BEFORE we can "have faith". But HOW are we gonna hear? (so we can "have faith", ya know) . . . well . . . according to the Bible, it is the Word of God that activates our hearing. So the Word comes first, opening our ears to genuinely hear, and then we can respond (faith). So the nature of the Word of God is such that it enables hearing (this hearing cannot be attained through our human choosing), leading to the fulfilling of that Word.

Isaiah 55:11 says that His (God's) Word ALWAYS accomplishes its (HIS) purpose: always succeeds! WOW! . . . I think this is worthy of a lot of further consideration, but you will hafta do that. I will too, but not in this writing.

So . . . the heavens and all of creation bring us The Word of God! Not, of course, the same as the Bible but (according to the Bible) THEY ARE THE WORD OF GOD!

How about stuff like tests or trials or tribulations? Could these be the Word of God to us? James (holy man of God who spoke as he was moved by the Holy Spirit) (James 1:21) seems to view such things as "the engrafted Word", able to save our souls . . . what about apostles, prophets, evangelists, pastors and teachers? Does the Word of God come to any of them? If so, and they pass it along to us, is it still the Word of God? How about Deacons? Or Preachers? (do THEY preach the Word of God?) Or older women teaching younger women? What do they teach 'em? Could that be the Word of God? Scriptures came about as holy men of God spoke as they were moved by the Holy Spirit. Are there any holy men of God living today? Women? If so, could THEY be speaking to us The Word of God? Today? How about God speaking to us personally? He used to, ya know: does He still? He said He doesn't change, so???

Matthew 4 is a record of Jesus being tempted by the devil (who wanted Him to turn some stones into bread). He must have been very hungry, since He had just gone through forty days without eating. (I'm pretty hungry after missing one meal). Anyway, satan tried to get Him to turn some stones into bread: He COULD, ya know: after all, He is the creator of everything that is created! But instead, He repeated what He had told Moses a few thousand years before, in Deuteronomy 8:3: Men do not live only by bread: rather, people live by every Word that the Lord (in every present moment) is speaking . . . WHOA! . . . Let's stop and think about that a bit! We are living . . . by the Word that God is speaking IN . . THIS . . MOMENT! (in EVERY moment of our lives)! Really! Please, let's not miss this! We who tend to think and plan and devise and try to control stuff . . . we tend to think THAT is living, but . . . (sad news folks): we can orchestrate and put our plans into action, and do stuff and we think that's living . . . but the problem is, it ain't true (if we believe the Bible, that is) . . . that AIN'T how we live! (it's only how we deal with stuff).

Well I'm starting to get the idea that God (the SAME God we read about in the Bible): THAT God . . . the ONLY real God . . . is continuing to be . . . in OUR lives, the SAME as He has always been! The scripture is a written account of God interacting with people: people like YOU, and people like me! The SAME God, being the SAME: TODAY! I am concerned that we make a big deal of Jesus dying on the cross about 2,000 years ago to forgive us our sins and to bring us eternal Life (and we SHOULD make a big deal about that: without that, we would have nothing . . . without that, we would all be dead!) And then of course we are captured by the news that He's coming back from Heaven to get us all and take us all back to Heaven with Him, where everything will be wonderful beyond our imagining . . . that, too, is certainly wonderful to think about!

My concern, however, is that we have somehow gotten deceived; seduced away from the reality of GOD IN OUR PRESENT LIFE . . . actively involved in the stuff of our lives in the same ways He did with those people we read about in the Bible And while this seduction and deception was happening, some of us decided to try to stuff God between the covers of our Bibles. Then we tried to make that Bible the ONLY word of God: we declared the Bible (NOT God Himself) to be the source for directions for living, and for the power to live it: BUT . . . God cannot be stuffed between the covers of ANY book, however wonderful that book may be. (And certainly the Bible IS a MOST wonderful book!)

Let's look at a couple of examples from the Bible about this. Think, for example, about Hosea (*you can read about it in his book: Hosea*). God had told Moses already how prostitutes should be treated: stoned to death, or burned, or some other equally disastrous treatment. That was the Torah; the scripture, which God had breathed; the Word of God to and through Moses. So what did God tell Hosea? hmmm . . . He told him to go find one of those and MARRY her and have children by her; then after she had left him and returned to her old life of prostitution, God told him to go find her and bring her back to his house again Does that seem right to you?

Then there was the time when the Israelites were murmuring and complaining and God sent a bunch of snakes (God's Word to snakes?) and the snakes bit a bunch of them so a whole lot of them died: remember that? (<u>Numbers 21</u>) Remember how previously God had told <u>Moses</u> (then through him to the people) that they were not to make any images of anything? But then He (God) told <u>Moses</u> <u>TO</u> make an image of a snake and put it up on a tall pole, so if someone had been bitten by a snake, and he just looked at that image on the pole, he wouldn't die? Remember that? Hmmm . . . First, the Word of God was <u>NOT</u> to make <u>ANY</u> images Then, the Word of God was <u>TO</u> make that image . . . wha ?

The thing is, ya see, that God . is . Lord . . . over <u>EVERYTHING</u>: at <u>ALL</u> times: even over the scriptures! When the Pharisees challenged Jesus and His disciples for breaking the Sabbath by picking and eating grain from the fields ON SATURDAY, He told them that He is Lord . . . Lord <u>OF</u> the Sabbath. And so it is that He <u>IS</u> Lord: THEN; in the future; and NOW! (today).

I really hope you are not getting the idea that I am trying, in ANY sense, to minimize the wonder; the great value; the magnificence of the scriptures . . . NO! . . . Rather, I am hoping to say that (as He has in the past, and since He doesn't change) we may have a clear understanding that He IS (and will be) speaking His Word to us: TODAY!

How might we be looking and listening to hear the Words He is sending to us? a partial list follows:

1. - Through the wonders of creation7.
2. - Through other brothers and sisters in Christ.
3. - Through true spiritual leaders, such as speakers, pastors, prophets, evangelists, and teachers, etc.
4. - Through circumstances that touch our lives, both delightful AND difficult.

5. -Through Him speaking to us personally: sometimes by an audible voice; sometimes by a whisper in our spirit (heart); maybe through a donkey, or a fish . . . and of course,

6. - Through the Scriptures. (the Bible, for most of us)

7. - Any OTHER way HE may choose to speak to us

So: shall we wrap this thing up? I thought you'd think so! OK, so here are some wrap-up thoughts:

Since we know that He upholds everything by the Word of His Power (Hebrews 11:3) . . . ALL THINGS . . . that includes YOU, ya know! He's upholding YOU in so many ways, such as the beating of your heart; the whole circulatory system; your breathing; your digestive tract: ALL your body's systems, controlled and maintained by His Word. (The "in-the-moment" Word of God)

Of course God does not speak to everybody the way He spoke to Moses or the prophets, etc. Many times He speaks to others (us) THROUGH such folks and of course, through the Bible. But we oughtta remember that at ANY time, in ANY situation, God CAN and MAY speak to us personally, and when He does that, it is no less the Word of God than the Bible is. HOWEVER His Word comes to us, it is TOTALLY . THE . WORD . OF . GOD!

We read (Hebrews 3:2,3,15, & 4:7) that whenever we hear the Word of God (His voice), we must be careful not to harden our hearts (not rebel against it) because if we do, we will never find His peace and rest. So Let's be looking and listening for His Word, and when it comes, in whatever way it comes, let's receive it, and enter into the good things He has planned for us!

I think it needs to be said that since God is Spirit, His WORD to us is ALSO Spirit. It can not ever be properly heard or understood by our human minds: only by our spirits, made alive by <u>Jesus</u>. Many have thought they understood "the Word", but they could only partially understand (misunderstand) the shell of it. <u>Jesus</u> told the religious leaders of His earthly days that they mistakenly thought that by searching the scriptures they would find eternal life, but those scriptures bore witness of Him: (<u>Jesus</u>), (<u>Who WAS and IS Life</u>) but they would not come to Him to actually <u>FIND</u> Life. (<u>Life is in Him Only</u>) There are, I have recently read, around thirty-eight thousand "christian" denominations in the world, all claiming their distinctives to be based in "the Word": all to some degree differing with each other, and not agreeing with each other regarding some or many beliefs. What's the problem here? Their primary problem (and ours, too) is that they (we) did not (because they <u>COULD NOT</u>) understand the spiritual reality couched in the "obvious" outer words of the Scriptures. So ANY Word of God, coming to us through ANY channel (we've looked at some of those in this writing) . . . ANY Word of God can ONLY be heard or understood by our spirits (and then only after God has made those spirits alive. Our natural abilities do not have the ability to perceive anything of God. Let's be careful NOT to depend on our own understanding! Let our dependence be on the Lord God Himself: <u>THE ONE</u> Who <u>WAS</u> in the past (that we read about in the Bible); <u>THE ONE</u> Who <u>WILL BE</u> in the future ("in heaven") . . . AND . . . <u>THE ONE WHO IS</u> . . . <u>NOW</u>: the <u>SAME</u> . . . <u>TODAY!</u>

Sin and Salvation . . . Part 1

Reconciliation

"For if, when we were enemies, we were reconciled to God by the death of His Son, much more, being reconciled, we shall be saved by His Life" Romans 5:10, KJV

Our salvation: HUGE ! So broad in the scope of what it accomplishes! So grandly magnificent in its effect on anyone and everyone who will believe it and receive it!

This scripture in Romans 5:10 shows for us two primary aspects of what we call "salvation". In this writing we'll take a look at the first: reconciliation. What IS reconciliation ? Why do we need it?

Well, as I see it, it's something that brings together two things or people that have become separated: it is a thing that takes care of or eradicates whatever caused the separation This involves, first of all, finding the cause of the separation; then naming it; then addressing it; then taking the necessary steps to correct or demolish whatever caused the separation.

When two friends have become separated, perhaps because of something one of them said or did, if both are willing to address and correct that something, then those two can be brought back to their friendship again: reconciled!

Likewise, a husband and wife who have become estranged

(separated) CAN be reconciled if there is a willingness to do what is needed . . . usually this (for the most part) involves the one who said or did whatever led to the break-up doing all he or she can to apologize or undo or make restitution. On the part of the offended one, it will require forgiveness.

With us and God, however it is a bit different, though of course there are similar elements.

With regard to US and GOD, it is WE who have done the "something" that caused the separation between Him and us. Yup . . . it was US: WE did it, and as it turns out, not only did we DO it, but we do not have any way to UN-do it. But what, exactly, was/is it that we DID ? Could it be we are still doing it? What IS it, exactly?

The Bible says it is SIN: our SIN has separated us from God. There! Ya feel better now? Now that ya KNOW what that something is that's been separating us from God? Now ya know! Right? . . . what? Ya don't know what "sin" is? Let's take a trip back to the garden: you know, THE garden: The FIRST garden, where our earliest ancestors lived: remember them? Adam, and his wife, Eve. I don't know their last names, but anyhow, there they were, just the two of 'em and God (and a bunch of animals of course, but that's another story.

So God lets 'em know that He's in charge which (at least at first) is fine with them. HE had already given them a bunch of fantastic stuff, ya know. God told 'em He hoped they'd enjoy the garden, and that He thought it would be great if they had a bunch of kids (children, ya know . . . not goats) . . . so they had a wonderful time, doing whatever they pleased, which made God very happy . . . "BUT", He said, "whatever you do, DON'T eat from that tree over there" (He pointed it out for them so there wouldn't be any doubt about which tree it was), "because if you

DO eat from it, you will die . . . that instant!" "It is <u>the tree of the knowledge of good and evil</u>, and it is <u>DEADLY</u>"

Now this is NOT (as many have taught) a situation where God made a rule, to test whether or not they would do what He said, and if they didn't, He would kill them. NO, that was <u>NOT</u> it! It was the tree . . . <u>THAT</u> tree; <u>the tree of the knowledge of good and evil</u> which, if they ate from it, would instantly kill them: instant death! (and that very tree is still living today, STILL DEADLY)

Apparently (I don't really remember) the animals talked back then, or at least one of them, because one day one of them came up to Eve and *basically told her that God was holding out on her when He told her not to eat from that tree. It isn't true that you will die like you think: God is keeping something wonderful from you: if you eat that fruit, you'll be LIKE God! You'll KNOW both good AND evil! Why should you let only God tell you what to do and what not to do? You can decide all that for yourself! Be your own boss Be king of the world!*

So anyway, that is basically what the animal told her . . . and after a while she believed that animal, and took some of the fruit from that tree (<u>the tree of the knowledge of good and evil</u>, you remember), and she ate some and gave some to her husband Adam, and HE ate it too . . . and guess what??? Right!!! . . . They both DIED ! On the spot!

They both died, but not their bodies: that took about another 900 years to happen. But they died in the exact moment they ate that fruit.

You've no doubt heard (about somebody or other) "they're running around like a chicken with its' head cut off". Can ya picture it? No? Shall I 'splain it to ya ? I COULD, ya know, having personally witnessed it in my childhood days. No? . . . ya don't WANT me to describe it for you? Well OK, I won't, but how about this: one day you go out and pick some flowers outta your garden; or some field; or the side of the road; or somewhere: then ya bring 'em home and stick 'em in a vase, or a glass, or a mason jar, or in SOMETHING and then you add some water and arrange them so they look BEAUTIFUL. Then ya put the whole arrangement some place where you can SEE it, and enjoy it: LOVELY !!!

But tell me . . . those flowers . . . are they alive? They LOOK alive, don't they? But the sad truth is, THEY'RE DEAD! Yup! Those flowers that look so good . . . are dead! . . . And ya know WHY they're dead? I'll tell ya. It's cuz the moment ya picked that flower, you separated it from its' life . . . Just like Adam and Eve, when they ate that fruit of that <u>tree of the knowledge of good and evil.</u> That act separated them from God, who was their Life; separated them from the only Life there is, the ONLY life for everything that exists! Separated . . . DEAD . . . Just like you and I were separated from God. We too were dead!

So . . . Adam and his wife Eve, choosing to feed themselves from that tree; <u>the tree of the knowledge of good and evil,</u> expelled God from their beings, where He HAD been dwelling: they expelled Him and therefore they expelled Life (though I don't think they knew they would be expelling Him: that animal didn't tell them THAT part). And so they died . . . that very moment . . . just like those flowers you picked, or the chicken without his head: dead!

AND . . . since from then on they existed another 900 or so years without Life (just like it took a while for your flowers to SHOW their death, and just like that chicken can run around without its' head) . . . since that point everything they touched was dead!; everything they produced, dead! Their kids (not goats, ya know) were born dead! Down through the centuries, to us: you and me, all born dead!

Not only that, but from the moment WE came into this world, we were taught and trained to "live" by our own "knowledge" of good and evil. THAT was THE sin that brought death to Adam and Eve, and it IS THAT SAME SIN that brings death to us today, because it bars entry to Life from our being. The issue is NOT that it's bad to have some concept of good stuff and bad stuff. The issue IS that operating with that as a basis for US running OUR lives is what excludes God (Life) from our being. We have been designed to Live with God filling our being and controlling all we think or say or do. Anything else is sin: THE sin! It's sin because God is not there and therefor Life is not there, and we are designed TO LIVE!

It is THIS SIN that Paul writes about when he tells us that there is ONLY ONE foundation for our lives: Jesus! And he writes to us that it is possible that we could do stuff all our lives (stuff that we consider "good",) and have it all burned up and destroyed in the end BECAUSE THOSE THINGS ARE NOT SOURCED IN GOD: it was not "on the only foundation". Jesus said that every tree that His Father had not planted will be uprooted and destroyed. He told how in the end there would be many who claimed to have done many miracles, and prophesied, and cast out demons "in His Name", and He would have to tell them to depart from Him: Their works were "iniquity". He did not "know" them: this means that *He had not been, in truth, the source of those works*. They probably spoke the words, "in Jesus' name", but they had never connected to Him AS GOD; the One Who was to direct all their steps. Jesus also said that anyone who was not (specifically) WITH Him was against Him. ("*while we were yet enemies*")

This is THE important matter to God: when He "shows up", He ONLY shows up AS GOD (wherever He is not barred). That means that HE is the one who is in charge always. He is to control <u>EVERYTHING</u>! This is NOT because He is an egomaniac, it is because He knows every aspect of how everything is made to be, and ONLY HE is the Life of every thing . . . every creature . . . His wrath sits on everything that is not filled with Him. Ya might say He is VERY MAD with all that, and VERY MAD at any person who insists on that.

So . . . this is <u>THE</u> sin for which Jesus died: all other "sins" that we normally think of when we use the word "sin", such as murder or rape or stealing or lying or having sex with someone when you're not supposed to . . . I suppose THAT list could go on and on . . . anyway, all THOSE sins come out of THAT sin: the sin of pushing God out of our life as God, and taking control of our life for our self, bringing death to our own being.

BUT . . . the GREAT news is that Jesus took THAT death (YOUR death, and MINE) into Himself, and because HE DIED THAT DEATH <u>FOR</u> us, and <u>IN PLACE OF</u> us, THAT sin (and all the other sins that come from it) have been paid for BY HIM, therefore no longer have THAT effect on us. (there is one specific sin which God is unable to forgive, but that's another story) . . . for all the rest of us, we are forgiven: therefore NOTHING (except that ONE sin) stands in the way of us being re-connected to God . . . to Life . . . WE HAVE BEEN RECONCILED! NO LONGER SEPARATED, BUT JOINED!

So do WE have any part in this? As I see it, there are a few internal things we need to do:

First of all we need to recognize the truth: recognize that we have been "running our own life" and that we are, therefore, dead . . . and that Jesus experienced OUR death FOR us.

THEN we repent (yup, there's that word we never like to hear) . . . we turn in our heart from thinking that we should "run the show" to wanting HIM to run our show.

Believe in our heart this truth, which means that we never depend on any other thing: no other possibilities for our reconciliation.

Receive God into our heart, AS GOD . . . TO BE GOD . . . OF US!

All four of these are done in our heart: <u>NOT</u> in our head.

One (maybe?) other thought: reconciliation to God is not just a nice thing He did for us, it is essential; necessary! Remember what our problem was? RIGHT!!! We were separated FROM God: separated FROM Life, so we MUST be reconciled in order to LIVE! BUT we <u>HAVE BEEN</u> reconciled, so death is no longer our problem! We can now go on to experience what Life is like under our NEW director!

Well, this has gone on long enough, don't you think? We'll explore some things about that new Life in a future writing . . . (it HAS to be future, cuz I haven't written it yet).

Sin . . . and Salvation . . . Part 2

Saved by His Life

"For if, when we were enemies, we were reconciled to God by the death of His Son, much more, being reconciled, we shall be saved by His Life"

Romans 5:10, KJV

(from Part 1) . . . we HAVE BEEN reconciled, so death is no longer our problem ! We can now go on . . . to experience what Life is like under our NEW director !

New Director: hmmmm . . . well yes, He's our new director, now that we have acknowledged that we have been running our own lives, which has been death to us (separation from God, as God); now that we see that this sin (that specific sin that has pushed LIFE out of our beings) is hateful to God because He desires nothing but LIFE for all His creation, and only He could do anything about it; that we have NO power at all to do anything about it. He DID do something about it: He sent His only begotten Son to this earth specifically to take on Himself to die the death that was OUR lot, INSTEAD OF US . . . now that we have repented of running our own lives; have believed and received God's provision for us, NOW we are re-connected to THE LIFE which we had been pushing out . . . reconciled . . . TO LIFE! Now we are no longer dead, but alive! Under new management! Truly, a NEW director: no longer us, but Him!

In this writing I am hoping to explore how this new LIFE begins, and how it increases all throughout our lives. He is not ONLY a director for us: not, like many have believed (and taught) that He sits on His throne "in the heavens" and tells us what to do and what not to do, and we hopefully obey Him. No . . . He is now no longer distant, remember? We've been reconciled! One thing about that Life (HIS Life) is, its nature is to increasingly expand, and to fill everything in existence (including you and including me)

So now the Life which He <u>IS</u> (which we HAD been keeping out) comes into our hearts: into the center; the core of our beings. We're no longer keeping Him out, but rather long for Him to live His Life IN us So He, Himself now lives IN US! HIS Life is now OUR life! We are no longer at all separated from Him, but UNITED with Him. NOTHING CAN SEPARATE US from Him who <u>IS</u> Love any more (unless for a time we take control of our own lives again, which still means separation in our experience) Of course even this cannot bring total separation, because THAT sin has already been forgiven We still experience the results of ourselves being "in control". (we think we're in control at those times). We go through whatever the consequences might be of us "being in control" of our own lives, and God-Life sits like a seed inside us, waiting for us to come into agreement once again that HE is to be "calling the shots". THEN once again His Life can resume its growth, as He intends. In the Kingdom of God, there is ONLY ONE King. (which is never any of us)

So . . . HIS LIFE now is at home in us: at first, a seed: HIS seed, destined to become a "new creation". It IS a new creation, which will become, as it grows, the specific new creature which He has already designed to be ME: the "me" which He had in mind for me since before the world began. He is NOT (as I've heard taught) making me into a "little Jesus". There is only ONE Jesus, and He came to our world when God Put His Life into a young virgin girl named Mary, and so Jesus came here and Lived His Father's Life and fulfilled His Father's plan (which plan resulted in OUR reconciliation AND our Life). And so He has now put His Life inside each of us who are His: in a sense, we are like Mary, but certainly not with the same design.

Anyway, now we have His Life inside us, and now, like ANY seed, it WILL grow. His Life inside an acorn will become an oak tree; inside a tomato seed will become a tomato plant with several tomatoes on it; inside an African violet seed will become an African violet plant with many blossoms for us to enjoy; inside a peach pit will become a peach tree with peaches on it (yum) etc., etc. And inside me (and you) it will become the true me (and the true you). Like ANY seed, however this seed inside me and you requires the proper environment in order to grow.

Question: do you (or I) know what this environment needs to be? I think the answer to THAT question for either of us is, "NO", we do not! . . . so . . . just like none of us knew how to get reconciled to God so we could LIVE, neither do any of us know HOW to grow. That, too, needs to be given to us, and that, too IS given to us by God (THE GOD Who now lives inside us).

So it all starts from the seed of His Life, now in us: but then what? As I see it, there are things OUTSIDE ourselves, all of which are orchestrated by God, and of course, His Life INSIDE us We've talked a bit about that, but what kinds of things does He orchestrate OUTSIDE us?

A new-born baby, in order to even COME TO birth, needs

to first of all spend quite some time inside his mommy. In there he receives nutrition from his connection with her and he has a warm, safe environment, and so he grows until it is time for him to leave that safe, warm place, and "be born". Do we know how that happens? Not exactly, though we have learned some things about it . . . BUT . . . what CAUSES him to grow is that life itself, which is a combination of the implanted seed (in our case, the seed of God's Life) AND the egg (in our case, the egg is us). BOTH are needed for the new life coming forth.

Then, for quite some time AFTER he is born, he requires constant, on-going care and attention: feeding; clothing; keeping him safe; bathing and cleaning, etc. He don't know how to do ANYTHING at first himself: all those things and more MUST be provided FOR him, BY others, and of course, even after those early months, he must be helped; trained; guided; sometimes disciplined throughout early childhood, teen age years, and early manhood: by someone or some ONES outside Himself: and so it is with us!

We'll take a look at some of the things OUTSIDE of us next, but first we need to consider that HE has NOT taken away our need to choose things, OR our capacity TO choose. In fact, we MUST choose! He does NOT force our growth on us so if we are to grow, it requires our cooperation! Every step of the way! But the POWER to choose, AND the power to actually DO what we choose (in our growing new Life) does NOT come from us, it is the nature of our new Life itself (HIMself). And just as in our human bodies, most of the things that go on inside us are occurring without our specific knowledge, like the operation of our circulatory system; our nervous system (I know, some of us are more "nervous" than others); our respiratory system; and all our other systems. We are not in touch with those things, and so it is with our spiritual beings: we have no need to be "in the know" about these things. They are taken care of by God, who also controls these things for our bodies.

But there are many other things, too, that are worth considering; things that reveal God's nature to us, like all the multiple things of His creation; the starry heavens; the wonders of how things grow; of all the green plants; of oceans; of deserts; of our own human bodies with their many "systems"; of the making of a rose; an iris blossom; a peach (yum); a puppy; a northern pike; an eagle; a parakeet . . . and that list is pretty much without end All these and many more speak to us (if we will pay attention) of the nature of our new director; our maker; our savior; our friend, and our Father: He Who now lives within us: of His creativity; of His limitlessness; of His power; of His absolute goodness . . . on and on.

Then there is the Church (I know, many of us are very disappointed with the Church . . . she is not yet, to be sure, all she is meant to be, with many failures, frustrations, and powerlessness, etc.) I think that, like each of us, she has not yet allowed THE LIFE to fill her. She yet has thought she knew how to "live" and how to grow. BUT there IS a church, and He IS helping her to grow into dependence on Him, and on His power. He IS doing it through all the weakness and failure that we see . . . as He IS in each of us . . . and IN His church are many who are equipped to HELP the rest of us become who we are destined to become. You can read quite a bit about that in the Bible: (in places such as Romans 12, I Corinthians 12-14, and in Ephesians 4).

And speaking of the Bible, it is FULL of things that speak to us about the nature of God (of our new Life); that show us what He is like; how He operates; what He loves and what He hates; what He has promised us, and so many other things.

The Bible is God speaking to us all through its many writers. In it are many instructions for how this Life we are now living LOOKS: specific directions for living it. If we believe what it says, however, it is NOT the only way God speaks today . . . a few of these I have mentioned above, all of which are filled and empowered by His Life (That Life that now lives IN US), but HOWEVER He speaks, His word is purposed by Him, for . our . good!

I have not yet spoken about His guidance: how He directs ALL OUR STEPS (except, of course, when we "grab the wheel") but even then He arranges our circumstances. He either causes or allows both good things that we love AND things that we call bad (remember our problem with thinking that we know what's good and what's bad? It didn't work, ya know: (still doesn't) So those things that we call bad; those things that hurt; painful: they come to us either FROM or THROUGH perfect Love, the nature of our new life. They give us an opportunity to allow the characteristic of that new Life to show up in our experience (characteristics like patience, or long-suffering, or real Love, etc.). These things are not produced in us except for through the hard stuff He allows: as one example, we would never learn to forgive others like He has forgiven us apart from going through some circumstance or other where somebody "done us wrong"

And of course He leads us into glorious times, when everything seems wonderful: when His Love pours over us and fills us, and when He blesses us with so many benefits and brings us things we love.

So, as one scripture tells us, He is at work inside us to make us able to agree with and to choose what He desires, and also to be able to DO those things, because they are done by HIS power. When He does "speak" to us, in whatever manner, it is so that "Word", with our agreement and cooperation and actions, will make us what we are made to be: HIS new creatures, not running our own lives but rather, becoming who we ARE because of HIS Life working inside us. We have been reconciled to Him, and now we are being saved by His Life flowing into and through us.

I think this is an ongoing and increasing process, going on now in our earthly lives, yes, but I am not sure that is all: I think, rather, that it goes on forever; grows forever! <u>"of the increase of His government . . . there shall be NO END"</u>!!!

Sin . . . and Salvation . . .
recap & postscript

In a recent note from a brother, he noted that there is such a wide variety of ways we all see or understand God . . . much like the story told of three blind men trying to describe an elephant, based on the part of the elephant they were touching . . . quite true for each of them, but as we all know, that elephant is much more than anything each of them were "in touch" with . . . so I think that as we think of "knowing God", this is an apt picture . . . as our brother <u>Paul</u> put it, "<u>we know in part</u>", or "<u>we see in a glass, darkly</u>" . . . for anyone to claim that they know all there is to know about God would be a gross deception, because He is so far beyond our abilities to fully "know".

Regarding the matter of THE SIN which we have been exploring, however, I am in hopes that I have presented a sufficiently clear writing. I am hoping that we can begin to see and understand that THE SIN which IS death. <u>THAT sin is the kicking of God off the throne of our life</u>, and that we do it when WE run our lives from the "<u>tree of the knowledge of good and evil</u>"; when WE decide for ourselves what to do and what not to do, based on "OUR knowledge"; when we are the "captain of our own ship"; when WE "run the show", etc., etc. When we take control, we wrest the control from God, and

THAT IS DEATH It is not that somewhere down the road it leads to death: it IS death.

And it is THAT sin (and THAT death) which Jesus took on Himself when He died on that cross: THAT sin; OUR sin and OUR death, He experienced in our place, and that is how He reconciled us back to God; how He cancelled everything that had been separating us from God and brought us back together with God! Now Gods' Life is IN US: a seed which will grow to cause us to become what (who) God originally intended us to be, living as God intends for us to live: God inside us, living His Life there . . . through us!

It is not true that God punishes us when we sin or that He made a whole bunch of rules, so He could swat us when we break one of them. The issue is that sin carries its own punishment. SIN CARRIES ITS OWN PUNISHMENT! which is some form of death: but Jesus bore that death! We stand forgiven !

Now we enter our adventure: as we come to begin to know His goodness, we first learn to value; then hunger for . . . Gods' way . . . in OUR life. This is a growing and learning experience, where we are continually in a "new" place. We truly do not know "what's next?" This, of course, puts us in a place of continuing trust in God: trusting Him; believing Him; depending on Him to do whatever needs to be done: a life free from anxiety and worry, resting in HIS doings and doing whatever He leads us to do, in total dependence on Him for everything that's needed: for us, and for everything and everyone we touch.

Sin and Salvation . . .
yet another look

Well OK . . . a brother has hinted that perhaps more could be written about the subject "Sin - vs - sins", so since (as you know) I am getting to be one who writes stuff, and since no-one to my knowledge has stepped up to do it, here I am, putting pen to paper (yes, literally: literal pen on literal paper: I know it don't look like that to you now, but that's how we're starting out, truly). So anyway, here I am writing more stuff, this time about Sin and sins.

Those of you who have read my other stuff will no doubt remember that I spoke about this in other writings under the heading(s) "Sin . . . and Salvation". (Reconciliation; Postscript & Recap; and Saved by His Life). It may be helpful to check those out, but here's another look:

It's pretty easy to identify sins: they're all over the place! BIG ones, ya know, like murder; rape; adultery; stealing; etc.; then there are others that aren't so big and bad (we think) like lying; cheating on our taxes; kicking the dog or cat; etc. (you get the idea), and there are the "socially acceptable" ones, like telling white lies; gossiping; and eating too much (yep, sorry darlin': that, too, is a sin) . . . I think you're with me here . . . if there IS an end to the list of possible sins, I don't know where it is: do you ? BUT . . . ALL that long list of sins springs from (has its source in) ONE Sin which is the root of all of it.

Adam & Eve: did THEY murder; rape?; commit Adultery?; Steal something from somebody? Did they bear false witness against their neighbor, or cheat on their taxes, or kick their pet? (I think they shouldda kicked that serpent.) How about telling white lies or gossiping or eating too much? NOPE: not ANY of these, at least not at first (maybe later), but at FIRST, they broke the first commandment: you know, "you shall have no other Gods before or besides Me" (yes, I know that commandment had not yet been "written", but that is what they DID). "How is that", you wonder? OK, well God specifically told them NOT to eat the fruit of that tree: you know, the tree of the knowledge of good and evil: "Don't eat from it", He said; "if you do, you'll die", He said, but did they listen? NO, they did NOT listen: they ATE. And when they ate what He had told them NOT to eat, they exalted themselves and their choices ABOVE God: they BECAME God, in Gods' place; and they died . . . right on the spot!

"But they only wanted to KNOW stuff", you say? "They just wanted to decide things for themselves", you think? "They wanted to be wise; make their OWN choices; be in charge of their own lives; be like God" (can anyone be like God by doing something He has said not to do?) "What's wrong with THAT?" you may be wondering: "doesn't EVERYBODY do that?" you ask? YES! EXACTLY, I reply: That IS what everybody does. We ALL DO want to be our own god, and that is why we are all in trouble: because we have ALL been "Making ourselves God". Another name for that is PRIDE: not necessarily that boastful, swaggering, arrogant looking kind of pride. Many times a sweet and humble appearing kind of pride that very "sweetly" demands its own way; and many other manifestations of that pride, and THAT is why we are ALL dead. <u>Adam</u> & <u>Eve</u> became <u>Adam</u> & <u>Eve</u>'s god; you were brought up to be your own god and so was I. Every time we assume the directorship of our own lives, we do THAT sin: <u>THE</u> sin which <u>IS</u> death. It is death because in ourselves we have NO LIFE: <u>LIFE MUST BE GIVEN TO US!</u> When WE take over, we kick God (as God) out of our lives, and <u>HE IS THE ONLY LIFE THAT EXISTS!</u> (there, I've said it)

    <u>Adam</u> & <u>Eve</u>, by eating the fruit of that <u>tree of the knowledge of good and evil</u>, Which God had specifically told them not to do, first replaced God with themselves, which opened up their beings and took in evil, (which they had no capacity or ability to handle). God HAD BEEN their Life: they only "knew": good. God HAD BEEN protecting them from all evil, but now they "knew" evil (which they had no capacity or ability to handle) and (though I don't think they knew this at that point) when they kicked Him out by assuming control, they kicked out their Life, and ever since, death has ruled on this earth: for <u>Adam</u> & <u>Eve</u> and for you and for me: Death has ruled until . . . UNTIL . . .

    UNTIL, that is, <u>Jesus</u>, a few thousand years later, left His Home in Heaven and came to this earth to be born and live as a man! The One who created everything that exists came and lived here on the earth He had created . . . about 33 years . . . then He allowed Himself to be beaten beyond recognition and then brutally crucified, spilling His Blood on the earth in the place of <u>Adam</u> & <u>Eve</u>; in the place of you . . . and me; in the place of, and on behalf of all of humanity. He willingly chose to go through all that, dying the death that was destined for all of us, <u>BECAUSE OF THAT SIN</u>: <u>THAT</u> sin: the sin of making ourselves God, which we all do. <u>THAT</u> sin which, by its very nature, pushes out the true and only Life that exists, leaving us without Life: dead . . . all of us! Separated by our own choice from God: from Life! This ONE sin . . . THE sin . . . always leads, without exception, to OTHER sins. To say it another way, if anyone commits ANY sin, it is because he/she has ALREADY committed THE sin!

So: John 3:16: *for God was SO MAD at the world for all their waywardness; for breaking all His laws; for not doing what He said to do and for doing what He said not to do, etc. etc., that He sent them all to hell forever.* Wait a minute . . . wha? No? . . . That's not what John 3:16 says? Well then, what DID He say? He SO LOVED the world? Ya mean that whole world that broke all His laws and hurt each other and disobeyed Him and wouldn't do what He said?; that insisted on doing things their own way?; That refused to let Him be God in THEIR lives? THOSE people?; YOU?; ME? He LOVED . . . ALL OF US? . . . in such a way that He GAVE us . . . His Son . . . to die the death that was ours? In OUR place?; FOR US?

So God was/is not mad at us people? Nope: not then; not now; not ever! S*o what's all the hoopla then about Him dying on the cross for us? If He ain't mad, what did He die FOR?* Ok, I'll tell ya . . . it was SIN that He died for: primarily THE SIN (and of course it follows that all the other sins get taken care of too). He died to pay the price of THAT sin: death!: the death that we ALL experienced when we sinned THAT sin. He gathered us all into Himself when He died, so because Jesus PAID our sin-debt (death), that death no longer has any power over us who believe. By paying that death penalty, He forgave THAT SIN (and every sin but one, which CANNOT be forgiven) OUR SIN IS (OUR SINS ARE) TOTALLY FORGIVEN: OUR DEATH DEBT IS TOTALLY PAID! HIS LOVE MADE IT SO!

So by Jesus' death on the cross, by believing Him:

1. - All my sin is completely forgiven.
2. - Every individual sin is completely forgiven.
3. - The second death no longer affects me.
4. - The barrier between me and God (which is THE sin) is demolished: I may freely come before God just the way I am, without any hint of fear or of shame.
5. - Because that barrier is torn down, the way is open for God to come to (into) me in any way that I will allow Him.

"For if, when we were enemies, we were reconciled to God by the death of His Son, much more, being reconciled, we shall be saved by His Life" Romans 5:10, KJV.

OK . . . so all this we've been talking about in this part of this writing has basically been about "reconciliation". Although this is absolutely necessary for our salvation (there is no chance of salvation apart from first being reconciled), it is only the beginning of our salvation. The door which was opened when Jesus demolished the barrier, (THE SIN, you remember) made a way for God to implant His very own Life in our beings, and this is what He did, though He planted it in seed form: the beginning of a whole new creation! It is THIS life, which is growing inside every one of us who have believed, which is our salvation. It (This Life) is the means by which we are saved: He, inseparably joined to me; forming the "new me"; being transformed day-by-day throughout this earthly life, one day to shed my earthly body, to continue my growth in the eternal Kingdom, forever! But wait . . . there's More!!!

(1)- The growth of this new creation will increasingly enable the "new me" to come to birth, all by His power and wisdom and after birth to learn the basics of life in the spirit realm, which is where the "new me" actually belongs. Also, all by His power and wisdom to grow and to mature: all this in similar manner to how we began and how we grew in our earthly life. The earthly is a dim shadow of the spiritual: a picture, though very dim.

(2)- Holy Spirit, now free to "speak" to me, helps me all along my way: My Helper; my Lover; my Guide; my ever-present companion all throughout my earthly journey. He helps me understand the many ways God is communicating to me: the heavens; the Bible; teachers; all the many wonders of "nature"; how to hear His Voice, etc. etc.

(3)- God Himself now orchestrates all the details of the growth of the "new me", bringing to me everything that is needed and good for the developing of this new "He-in-me" creature which He has designed.

    a. - This includes many wonderful encounters with Him, and many wonderful gifts which we both love and enjoy.

    b. - This also includes bringing us through many not-so-enjoyable circumstances and difficult people, and disciplining us (pain) which we neither love NOR enjoy. (But which is equally if not more important to our growth)

This is the fuller meaning of "Grace". We are no longer under law, but under Grace. This means we are in the place where God is in charge of our lives in every way; every aspect; nothing is, any more, a matter of OUR choices. (Remember, it was OUR choosing that got us in trouble, and we will not be truly fully saved until ALL choices are HIS, and until we stand in agreement with whatever He has chosen for us.) To say it another way, doing things OUR way removes us from the sphere of Grace.

One more thing: it is extremely important for us to understand that this wonderful Salvation plan is NOT about improving the "natural us"; NOT about some sort of renovation project; NOT a restoration plan or a rehab program. It is about the creation of an <u>ENTIRELY NEW ENTITY</u> . . . <u>a totally NEW life</u> . . . <u>Jesus</u> took that old thing we thought was life but which actually was death into Himself on that cross, and that old "me" (which <u>WAS dead though I didn't know it</u>) is now "doubly dead", and now all God is about; the only focus of His ministry to "me" is to the "new me". Nothing of the "old me" is able to enter eternal Life (to "get into heaven"): only the "new me" can enter!

It is all about: it <u>IS</u> . . . <u>CHRIST IN US</u> . . . It is about <u>living IN OUR NEW LIFE, and living OUT OF THAT NEW LIFE</u> !

<u>RECONCILED! . . . AND SAVED!</u>

Forgiveness (a teaching outline)

All scriptures in this outline are KJV

<u>"Giving Out What God is Putting In"</u>

- <u>We are designed to operate totally out of God as the source.</u>
  - <u>James 1:17 – "every good and perfect gift is from above"</u>
  - <u>Romans 11:36 – "from Him, through Him, and to Him are ALL things"</u>
- <u>The heart of ALL sin is "apart-ness" from God.</u>
  - <u>Genesis 3 – the fruit of the tree of the knowledge of good and evil is DEATH.</u>
  - <u>Ezekiel 18:4 – "the soul that sins WILL DIE"</u>
  - <u>Romans 3:23 – "ALL have sinned" (so, ALL are dead)</u>
  - <u>Romans 6:23 – "the wages of sin is death"</u>
- <u>Our hearts want to judge (analyze, assess, etc), think, and act ON OUR OWN</u>
  - SOOOOO . . . we sin: cause death; to ourselves, and to others.

<u>BUT</u>

(Because Jesus died on the cross, paying the penalty for ALL our self-originating activity)

- Romans 6:23 – "the Gift of God is ETERNAL LIFE"
- II Corinthians 5:17 – 19 –
  - We are NEW CREATURES in Him
  - God is RECONCILING the world through Jesus
  - The work of reconciliation is given, entrusted to US, in Him
- Luke 6:38 – whatever we give, we get back IN GREATER MEASURE
  - When we give, we are given to.
  - Matthew 5:7 – when we give mercy, we get mercy
  - Matthew 6:14 – when we give forgiveness, we get forgiveness
  - James 2:18 – when we give judgement, we get judgement without mercy
  - Mark 11:26 – when we do NOT forgive, WE WILL NOT BE FORGIVEN
  - Matthew 18: 23-35 – not only that, we will be TORTURED

- Matthew 18:35 – we must forgive FROM OUR HEART

- Forgiveness:
  - NOT a feeling, but IS a chosen act, PAYING THE PRICE
  - NOT glossing over something, but IS facing the damage, paying, releasing
  - NOT letting off the hook, but IS turning justice over to God
  - NOT continuing under abuse, but IS handling situation without vengeance
- OUR forgiveness is limited in scope, but within our own realms of experience

- In Ephesians 4:32 we read, "but be KIND to one another; TENDERHEARTED; FORGIVING one another, even LIKE GOD, WHO FOR JESUS' SAKE,HAS FORGIVEN you" . . . a freer translation might be, "but as for you, I want you to be kind to one another, and tender toward them in your heart . . . and I want you to forgive one another in exactly the same way and to exactly the same extent that God the Father has forgiven you in response to the sacrifice of His Son Jesus, and for His sake".

- In order to offer that kind and that depth of forgiveness, it is necessary for us to go through the same steps that God has gone through, so we can arrive at the same destination.

- I think it is important to have Jesus' sacrifice in OUR hearts as we approach this issue for those who have wronged us: that is, that He HAS ALREADY forgiven THEM, and we are setting ourselves in that same line, agreeing with Him, because He has already done it all both for US AND for THEM! When WE do the steps, we leave the person who wronged us in HIS hands. HE will take care of whatever vengeance or discipline that person needs, NOT US!

Taking Offense

Have you noticed how EASY it is to take offense? I mean, so MANY opportunities present themselves to me, with amazing frequency! So many people do things that they should NEVER have done, and to ME of all people! Or else they don't allow ME to do what I want to do: UNTHINKABLE !

Don't they realize how important a person I am? How wonderful? How intelligent? How wise? How supreme are my judgements? How talented? How god-like? How supremely well-equipped I am to assess all situations and dictate how everyone ought to run their affairs? Really!!! How DARE they treat me this way??? How could I NOT be offended?

And since I can hardly be blamed for being offended in these situations, what can I do other than separate myself from those others who have brought such pain into my life? And surely I would not be blamed if I carried a little grudge against them until they at least recognized their error: until they at LEAST said they were sorry.

The PLUS side of all this, at least at first, is that I get to review in my own mind all those wonderful things about myself that I have just mentioned, and rehearse in my mind just how low those others are. I can just let all that stir around in my mind, establishing the truth of it more and more firmly (in my mind), and justifying it with increasing clarity, and of course I have the satisfaction of not being faced with those characters who have done this to me. AND I can get a few friends to agree with me absolutely, helping me be my wonderful self (in my own mind).

The NEGATIVE side is, of course, that I am more limited as to with whom I can peacefully associate, but since they are THAT sort of people, that's not really THAT negative. The OTHER negative is that God don't like me to take such offenses, or so He seems to say: but He don't know how BADLY I have been treated (He was most likely paying attention to some OTHER person or situation: and anyway, He will forgive me: won't He?

What? Really? He don't like it? How can I believe THAT?

OK, well He said a few things, which I suppose He means:

In one place He tells us to love everybody else by treating them the way I would like to be treated: hmmmm . . . would I want to be forgiven for the stuff I do? Maybe I have never done anything that really needs forgiving . . . hmmmm . . . really? or maybe I HAVE done some stuff that I'd like God to forgive me for (dangling participle, I know: sorry) Ya know, He SAID He'd forgive me for ALL my sins (Except for one, which I know I have NOT committed) . . . and anyway, MY stuff is tiny: pretty much insignificant. Not that I'm ungrateful that He's forgiven me, but REALLY: what this guy done to me is MUCH worse than anything that I have done. How could He really expect me to forgive that HUGE thing that HE done to ME? He must not have meant that scripture to apply to ME when I have been SO badly mistreated by that guy, did He? Really? . . . DID He?

Well in another place He said to forgive one another the way He has forgiven me . . . which was how, exactly? You mean like TOTALLY? No matter how grave the offense was? Or how many times he has offended? No more demand for justice? No demand to pay for what was done? No feeling sorry for myself?

Really? No holding any of it against that guy, even when he has not even said he's sorry? Same as the way He has forgiven me: hmmmm . . . no grudge? . . . hmmmm . . .

And in still another place He tells us to consider others better than ourselves. Oh c'mon: Really? THAT guy? BETTER than ME? How in the world am I supposed to do THAT? OBVIOUSLY he is NOT better than ME! Indeed! How could I even THINK of considering him better than ME? And then He also says not to think of myself more highly than I ought to think: hmmmm . . . could THAT be the problem? really? That I think too highly of myself? Could it be?

And THEN He says that if I don't forgive EVERYBODY freely from the heart, then HE will not forgive ME? That HE will turn me over to the torturers? My goodness, that sounds really serious! NOT forgive ME? Torturers? All because I don't wanna forgive that clod? Just because of a little grudge? Well, HE did say these things: Maybe I gotta do a little re-thinking???

Cost Of Forgiving

Forgiveness is Very costly, of that there is no doubt. Think about it: if you lent a friend $5,000.00 and that friend was, for whatever reason, unable or perhaps even unwilling to pay you back, you are out $5,000.00.

At this point you have some options: you could:

1. - Plot some sort of revenge: if he (or perhaps she, but from now on I'll just use "he") doesn't pay you back, you could, for example, cut the tree down behind his house and make it fall on his roof, causing damages that hopefully would cost him at least $5,000.00, or if it didn't, then you could dump a load of dirt in his swimming pool, and if that still wasn't enough . . . well, you get the idea . . . so many possibilities. . . . Or . . .

2. - Just get good and mad, and have nothing to do with him ever again. That'll show him!!! And if that causes problems with some of his relatives, well too bad. They're probably on HIS side, anyway, so they SHOULD suffer too, don't ya think?

3. - (this is a popular one) Just let his injustice sit in your gut and simmer; rehearse in your mind what a rotten person he is; how miserably he has treated you, and how much he deserves to be punished, and how much you hope he will "get what's coming to him"

Just wondering, though: did any of that get your $5,000.00 back? No? Didn't think so. So you can't find any way to get that $5,000.00? Guess not, eh? So it looks to me like no matter what you do, you are still out that $5,000.00. So what exactly DID you get that benefited you? A nice knot in your gut whenever you thought about it? A nice grudge? Some nice bitter thoughts? Satisfaction, that you were able to think of things to "get him back"? Satisfaction that at least you made HIS life miserable? Really? Hmmmm . . . ??? . . . of course you COULD . . .

4.- Forgive him. FORGIVE HIM??? Yeah, you know, like Jesus did for you . . . or did you think Jesus only forgave you LITTLE stuff? Certainly not anything like that $5,000.00, right? Is that what you really think?

And then He says that we need to forgive that guy LIKE HE FORGAVE US: well how DID He forgive us? For a FEW things? Partially? Which parts did he forgive? And which parts did He NOT forgive? Seems like that might be important for us to figure out. (if we really want to do what He says) But HE says ALL sins (except for one, and that one has nothing to do with money) are forgiven by Him. So if we decide to forgive that guy like Jesus forgives us, what will that involve? What did it involve for Jesus?

Well, it involved Him PAYING the debts that we owed. In His case, it involved dying. (in our place)

So what about that guy who wronged me out of $5,000.00? If I were to forgive him, what would that involve for me? I suppose, paying that $5,000.00 myself, so now he doesn't owe me any money any more? Is that it? Well actually, that's NOT it: at least not ALL of it. If we want to do it like Jesus did it, then we will go BEYOND merely paying his debt ourselves: we will LOVE that guy (cuz HE says so) and we will also look for ways to do GOOD to that same guy. (cuz HE says so)

So: should I loan him another $5,000 bucks if he should ask me? I'm thinking probably not, but it might be possible. But I will not know whether or not until after I have forgiven him like Jesus did for me: then I will see and understand clearly what should lie in my future with that guy. Then I will begin to understand that THAT guy is messed up: LIKE ME. (of course not in the same way as him: not with owing money, or anything, but in my own "special ways")

So yeah, forgiving is costly: sometimes VERY costly! So are you willing to do it? For THAT guy? Absorb the loss, and even go beyond?

Cost of <u>NOT</u> Forgiving

Well OK, we've thought about the cost OF forgiving, but what about NOT forgiving? Does THAT have a cost? Well, let's think about that:

Can ya not forgive and be at peace, inwardly? No? Thought not: so there's ONE cost.

How 'bout when ya think about the wrong he did you? Can you keep from being upset? Ya LIKE being upset? Not really? So there's ANOTHER cost.

Then there's thinking about getting even some way: can you avoid doing that? How does it make ya feel? Not so hot? Another cost.

And thinking how much better than that scum YOU are: well that's not so bad, is it? (unless you think what God says is important: you know, about PRIDE and all that stuff. He doesn't seem to like that pride stuff much, does He?) Of course if you don't care much what HE thinks, then this ain't so bad, is it? So ya won't have to worry about that, at least until judgement day, if there IS a judgement day, so maybe ya won't need to worry about THAT cost, at least not right now.

How about sleeping? Does thinking about that keep ya up at night? Maybe not, but if so, there's another cost.

And what about how this refusal of yours to forgive affects OTHER people?; Your relationships with those who used to be your friends? Relatives? How about your kids: do ya think it won't affect THEM? MORE cost !

So ya don't care all that much about THOSE costs? Ok then, do ya care about what GOD says about not forgiving? Ya don't know what He says? Let me tell ya: HE says that if you don't forgive that dolt (and every other obviously inferior person) for what he (or she) done to you <u>FROM YOUR HEART</u>, THEN <u>HE WON'T FORGIVE YOU.</u> Really? Yep, really! Do ya really want to pay THAT cost? Really?

Let me explain something here: the heart of our Gospel is that <u>Jesus</u> died to provide forgiveness for EVERYONE. (if they would only believe it) That means that HE has declared that dolt forgiven: so now, YOU want to declare that guy UNFORGIVEN ? YOU have more say in that matter than GOD? . . . hmmmm . . .

But it doesn't stop there: when you refuse to forgive, then you, by your actions, are telling God that you don't believe in that forgiveness stuff, and if you don't believe in that forgiveness stuff then you haven't believed in it for yourself either, (even if you think you have) . . . and God will honor you not believing, as He will honor any other belief you hold (as long as we are living this earthly life). But since you are not believing in Jesus' sacrifice for YOUR sin, you will not receive His forgiveness, even though He has paid the cost for it: for you, AND for that dolt! <u>You may not have it if you deny it to anyone else</u>. What do you think about THAT cost?

Maybe there are OTHER costs, too: I just haven't thought of 'em just now: but isn't this enough, Really?

When To Forgive

Prompted by a brother's question about whether or not we ought to forgive a person unless he/she has repented, I have done a fairly extensive study of the scriptures that address that issue, and here is what I think I see: Many scriptures clearly tell us to forgive, but perhaps the most impactful (to me) is the section near the end of <u>Matthew 18</u>, ending with "unless you forgive . . . from the heart . . .

So it seems to me that there is no option other than to forgive that slug immediately and totally, FROM MY HEART!

It is true, most definitely, that in order for forgiveness to be meaningful to a person, that person must recognize that he/she has done something that needs forgiving. The question might be whether or not "I" should be the one to attempt to make him/her aware of his/her transgression, because in most cases, as Jesus said, "<u>they know not what they do</u>". My thought is that usually (though perhaps not always) it will not be "I" who is given the ability to enlighten that one, especially if it has been a transgression against ME. My given portion, as I understand it, is to immediately forgive them.

Having then forgiven them, many times a statement such as "when you did "xxxxxxx" I felt "zzzzzzz": a non-judgmental statement of our truth will effect a form of repentance on the spot, and help the person see what they most likely did not see previously, to repentance: to an expression of forgiveness, to the opening of the way to restoration and wholeness.

As with us and the Lord, Who forgave us "before we existed", so it needs to be with us: always <u>FIRST</u> forgiving. Then, whatever may need to be ministered after that can be done with a clean, clear, uncluttered heart: my own thoughts and emotions will not then be blocking the effectiveness of any other action we might subsequently take, and the possibility of "gaining our brother" is greatly increased.

There are times, I believe, when we may truly, based on Jesus' payment of all manner of sin, declare to a person, "your sins are forgiven" At the direction of Holy Spirit, this can be a powerfully liberating thing to say to them . . . <u>AT THE DIRECTION OF HOLY SPIRIT</u> . . . and there are times when we can tell a person, "I forgive you", but this will only be meaningful, I believe, when the person has acknowledged their offense, either saying they are sorry or perhaps asking for forgiveness.

In the truest sense, as David says in the Psalms, sin is a thing which is only and always "against God" ("<u>Against Thee and Thee only have I sinned</u>", He said to the Lord). Yet we all have a circle of responsibility unique to each of us, within which we are to operate, extending God's love within that circle Many other issues we might hear about are not ours to address: those are within another's sphere of responsibility, and of course ALL these spheres are under the care of the Lord. (including "my" circle)

We have ALL been given the responsibility to PRAY regarding anything about which we become aware, but usually our responsibility ends there, in the "prayer room" (In recognition that all sin is against God, and only God), and any other thing which ought to be done should be done in response to what we hear in prayer.

So yes, a person needs to be brought to a place of repentance before they can experience the benefits of forgiveness, but the forgiveness needs always to be accomplished <u>FIRST</u>. The price needs to be paid and the cost absorbed. (as Jesus did) Then the way is open for restoration: reconciliation has been accomplished on the part of the offended, and the way is opened for the needed steps toward full restoration. We will have, then, as Jesus said, "gained our brother", which is our goal . . . our ONLY goal.

Why Do We <u>Not</u> Forgive ?

Why do we not forgive? hmmmm . . . I suppose there are a lot of reasons, but I'll share some I'VE thought of.

1. - We don't wanna pay the cost.
2. - We don't realize we ARE ALREADY paying the cost, whether we think we are or not.
3. - We think if we forgive him it means we hafta think he didn't really hurt us.
4. - We think if we forgive him, that gives him a right to hurt us again.
5. - We think if we forgive him, that means he's "off the hook", so to speak . . . and we CERTAINLY don't want THAT!
6. - We think we don't need to think about what God thinks.
7. - We think He (God) didn't mean what He said about not forgiving us if we don't forgive that clod.
8. - We think what God said about it doesn't apply to US, in OUR situation.
9. - We don't think there <u>IS</u> a God: ESPECIALLY not one who expects us to forgive that dirt-ball.
10. - We think what WE think is more important than what God thinks.
    AND (I think this is the most significant one)

11. - We don't really believe that God has already forgiven US: totally; completely for ALL we have done, or ever WILL do.

12. - We don't really believe we have much of anything to be forgiven FOR: we're really not all that bad: certainly NOT as bad as that scum-bag.

So we could have a bunch of reasons not to forgive . . . are any of them any good?

After Forgiving . . .

OK, so now I have forgiven that low-down-dirty-rotten PERSON for what he done to me, so NOW what? What ELSE am I expected to do?

What? I've got a bad attitude? After what he done to me? What the heck am I S'POSED to think? Should I be all lovey-dovey, and tell him what a sweet, precious treasure he is? I DON'T THINK SO! And don't expect ME to do anything NICE to that worm: ain't gonna happen!

You say the Lord has different ideas? Really? O — K . . . I suppose I better listen to whatever HE says . . . go ahead . . . lay it on me.

The Lord wants me to PRAY for that clod? I'll pray . . . I'll pray that he trips over his dog and breaks his arm . . . sure I'll pray. No, you say? Not that kind of prayer? I'm s'posed to pray for something GOOD to happen to him? Well maybe I could think of something good to pray for him but I certainly won't FEEL like I want something good for him! You think my feelings will change after a while? I don't see HOW, but I'll give it a try.

So you're saying the main thing the Lord wants is for me to LOVE that slug?; that forgiving him is only the BEGINNING?; that He actually wants to HELP the guy, and He wants me to be the main character to get that done? How is that supposed to happen when I don't even WANT to help him? I WILL want to help him after my feelings change? I don't believe <u>THAT'S</u> gonna happen any time soon.

You seem to be thinking that it's Gods' nature to forgive everbuddy, and that He has put His nature in ME? So HE will actually do the loving THROUGH me if I will let Him? Well OK, I'm willing to try that, but I sure don't see how it's gonna work: the stuff he done to me is still there, ya know. We haven't resolved ANYTHING: how can I LOVE him when all that stuff is still there? Forgiving is ONE thing: LOVING is quite another, as I see it!

The Lord will show me how to deal with this stuff? Really? You say He has a solution to EVERY problem? This I gotta see!

But what if I blow it? That's pretty likely, ya know. This stuff you're telling me is VERY different from everything I've ever thought. Even if He DOES tell me what to do, it's likely that I won't DO it very well. He'll forgive ME for all that, and keep trying to get me to understand it and actually DO it? And He has a way to make all this stuff come out good, even after I've blown it? That sounds really far out to me, but here goes!

All right: that's MY story. Gonna give it a go: what about YOU? What's YOUR story?

Sometimes We Discover Stuff

(when we finally set out to forgive someone)

When we decide to set our hearts to forgive a person, we often discover things we were not expecting:

Sometimes we find they had no clue they were doing anything to hurt us.

Sometimes, that even when they DID intend to hurt us, they still didn't actually know what they were doing (like those who crucified Jesus, or those who stoned Stephen to death).

Sometimes, that doing stuff like that was how they grew up: believing that life was SUPPOSED to be lived that way, and they didn't know any other way to act.

Sometimes we discover that they didn't even DO what we thought they did. We have misjudged them and falsely accused them. It is then that we discover that the real issue is not forgiveness: the real issue is that we have a need to "repent" of our own false judgement and the pain it has caused. THAT is what is actually called for . . . NOT forgiveness.

We might discover that we are doing the same thing (or something very similar) ourselves . . . hmmmmmm . . .

Or we might just BEGIN to discover that we are not so much better than them than we thought we were.

Sometimes we find that the real issue is that we didn't get our own way! (Can you believe that?) That things didn't go the way we wanted, and we got mad. And when that happens, another discovery looms: WE are the actual problem, and we gotta get over our bad self!

We might just BEGIN to discover just how prideful we are: oh my! Hmmmmmm . . . maybe there's more to this forgiveness thing than we thought?

How to Forgive

In <u>Ephesians 4:32, KJV</u> we read "<u>*but be ye kind one to another;*</u> <u>*tender-hearted, forgiving one another even as God, for Christs'*</u> <u>*sake hath forgiven you*</u>" . A more free translation might be: "<u>but</u> <u>as for you, I want you to be kind toward each other, and tender</u> <u>toward them in your heart, and I want you to forgive each other</u> <u>in exactly the same way, and to the same extent that God the</u> <u>Father has forgiven you because of the sacrifice of His Son</u> <u>Jesus, and for His sake</u>".

In order to offer that kind and that depth of forgiveness, it is necessary for us to go through the same steps that God has gone through, so that we can arrive at the same destination. An outline of these steps follows (as clearly as I can understand):

1. - With careful, all-inclusive detail, completely assess the offense, omitting nothing.
2. - Without the smallest reservation, and omitting no detail, fully charge the offending person or people for that offense.
3. - Determine, in full, what the cost to you <u>IS</u> for that offense.
4. - Charge the offending person or people the complete cost to you of that offense.

5. - You, yourself, pay the entire debt which you yourself have reckoned . . . completely . . . in full . . . with no reservations.

NOTE: *it is not possible to escape having to pay the cost of someone's offense. You can pay it with anger, bitterness, resentment, self-pity, hatred, strife, etc. in your heart or you can pay it FREELY, FROM YOUR HEART, in God's power, in recognition of the great debt that God has already paid for YOUR offenses*

6. - Make a formal declaration that you are no longer holding the offending person or people responsible for paying that debt, based on the fact that you have already freely and totally paid it yourself.
7. - In your own mind, set that offending person or people absolutely free and refuse to ever again hold them responsible to pay for that offense.

Now YOU are free YOURSELF! Be free . . . and stay that way!

Spurtchial Worefar part 1

Some basic thoughts

OK, OK . . . relax children . . . yeah, I know, but as you may already have guessed, I'm wanting to talk about the battle all of us are fighting in. (whether we know it or not) Ya see, as most of us know, God has gone to great lengths to pay a horrendous price: the beating and the death of His Son by crucifixion, to make it possible for us to believe in Him and find Life; true Life; eternal Life, and He continues to draw us moment by moment by His Spirit to increasingly experience that Life even while we are "living" our earthly "life". THAT is, by far, the most important thing any of us could hear and understand and believe and receive.

Then there are satan and his "minions", whose sole purpose is to destroy life: to bring death to all that God has created: All humanity. (which means he wants to kill us all) His method; his tactic is deception, either by outright lies or by partial truths designed to warp THE truth and thereby mislead any who listen, and by that lead us away from Life, to death.

The bad news is that ALL of us have listened to his lies and acted on them: we have ALL been deceived, and we have ALL died . . . UNTIL we believed on Jesus, that is . . . which is how and when we entered into REAL Life (out of our death). For those of us who have believed, He (God) has given us His Own Life which will complete our "salvation".

Now, both God and the enemy are using the same basic tactic to reach their goals (as we said, Gods' goal is to bring us to Life and grow that Life, and the enemys' goal is to destroy that Life, either by blocking us from believing the good news of Jesus or by preventing any growth in that new Life after we HAVE received it. So since (as one of the Proverbs tells us) "as a man thinks in his heart, so IS he"; and since Gods' desire for us is to bring us to Life; and since the enemys' desire is to destroy it, they both seek to affect our thinking: yup, our thinking . . . the reason? Because by affecting our thinking, our "us" is affected. In this case either toward Life or away from Life (toward death). It is the state of our "BE" - ing that is at stake. This is truly a Life-or-death matter!

To Eve, the enemy spoke a combination of outright lies and partial "truths", trying to get her to believe them, and persuade her to act apart from God which, as we all know, he was successful in doing, and this believing which Eve did resulted in her death (and consequently the death of all humans since). He aimed at her "MIND": where her thinking took place: he affected her thinking, which brought about her death, which brought about the death of all of us since.

"For we wrestle not against flesh and blood, but against principalities, against powers, against the rulers of the darkness of this world, against spiritual wickedness in high places"- (Ephesians 6:12), KJV. . .

the Amplified version says it this way: *"For we are not wrestling with flesh and blood [contending only with physical opponents], but against the despotisms, against the powers, against [the master spirits who are] the world rulers of this present darkness, against the spirit forces of wickedness in the heavenly (supernatural) sphere"*

I'd like to re-say it something like this: we . . . <u>ARE</u> . . . wrestling, but we are <u>NOT</u> wrestling against people (human beings) . . . rather, <u>we ARE wrestling against the whole horde of evil spirits of all sorts</u> who have "<u>exalted themselves against the knowledge of God</u>".

These scriptures point out a few things that I believe are vital for us to begin to understand:

1. - We <u>ARE</u> wrestling: I think many, if not most of us do not have any significant awareness of the assault on our beings being waged by the horde of evil spirit beings. We have, as it were, been "pinned to the mat" by that assault without even knowing it, and therefore we have not engaged in any effort to resist. Blinded minds, one scripture calls it: we don't really see the enemy with any clarity. Most of us want and try to "do good", of course, and I don't believe there are any who want to submit ourselves to that evil. Yet, whether or not or to what degree we are aware of it, we <u>ARE</u> involved in this war.

2. - (VERY important, I think) This is <u>NOT</u> a struggle (a wrestling) with other people! This is difficult for most of us because it is, after all, how we become aware of a problem: the way someone acted and/or spoke plainly tells us of something unacceptable to us: She was mad at me, or she refused to make me a dinner, or he cursed at me, or lied about me, etc. etc. We SAW it with our own eyes, for goodness sake, or heard it with our own ears: <u>OBVIOUSLY</u> the problem is with him (or her), right? . . . <u>WRONG!</u> . . .
    Because . . .

3. - It is a SPIRITUAL issue: that is, it is a happening instigated by SPIRIT beings and affecting him or her. This IS to be resisted and overcome, but NOT AGAINST him or her: he or she has been lied to or deceived by those evil beings, and he or she is a victim of their attack, and when we attack him or her, we make THEIR mess much worse! We MUST learn where to aim our attack if we hope to succeed! WE are FOR him or her (never against them), and against those evil ones that have captured them for a season.

This is called "spiritual warfare" (see, I DO know how to spell it), which first of all means that it is a warfare initiated and carried out by Holy Spirit, Who is living inside all of us who are His. We become involved in this warfare only as we are submitted to Holy Spirit leading and directing each "battle". It is a SPIRIT thing, and there can be no success when we "come against" our fellow-humans: only greater problems.

Our direction, for EACH (every) battle needs to come from the Lord Who (alone) knows the battle plan. This warfare is never to be undertaken in our human strength or our great human wisdom, and NEVER without the specific instruction of the Lord. (Who lives in our heart.) I am aware of a teaching going around out there that because we are "saved" and Jesus lives inside us and He died so we could have everything we want, etc. etc., that we now have full authority to heal everybody that's sick or raise the dead or cast out devils wherever we meet them, etc. etc. This is a very dangerous false teaching! We are not given "blanket" authority to do any grandiose deeds we think we'd like to do: like Jesus, (while on earth), we are to go about doing ONLY what Father is doing. Contrary to popular thought, Jesus did NOT heal everyone that was sick (though

He DID in some regions; He did NOT cast out every demon that crossed His path; and He did NOT raise every dead person back to life. He did NOT walk on water every day, nor did He feed crowds of thousands with a few fish and a couple of loaves of bread every day. He did those things when and where He saw Father doing them, and that is OUR business also: saying and doing only what Father is about in all our situations. I personally know of several folks who (like the seven sons of Sceva, recorded in the book of Acts) attempted spiritual warfare without being given authority or direction, and suffered similar or worse results. Please do not do it! Not one of us is equipped to deal with these evil ones on our own. We MUST have God-Life flowing from Him through us in each moment if we are to have success in that moment.

Brother Bob contributes this:

"Jesus came to destroy ("bring to naught") (the Amplified version adds this: undo; destroy; loosen and dissolve)the works of the Devil: the works the devil [has done](I Jn. 3:8). How He does this is seen in the accounts of Chapters 4 of Matthew and Luke. As the admonition (above) makes clear, we are tempted to think that we first must feel an infusion of power or authority and then act on that power. Jesus did not do this. He first was led by the Spirit of God into the wilderness to fast. Jesus was in a weakened condition when Satan spoke to Him. Jesus' resisting of the Devil took the form of refusing to act apart from His Father.

Satan's deception played on an acknowledgement that Jesus is the Son of God in order to coax Him into acting independent of the Father, relying instead on His position as Son of God. Jesus responded each time out of the reality that He is indeed the Son of God and does not act independent of the Father".

So to sum up this writing, in addition to the paragraphs just above, let's be clear that we are under siege: <u>ALL</u> of us; it is a SPIRITUAL siege, NOT a physical, human siege; the siege may come against you personally or a spouse; a friend; a pastor; a church: it comes against <u>ALL</u>, and our weapons for standing and/or defeating the evil ones are SPIRITUAL weapons: NOT human wisdom or plans or abilities.

Spurtchial Worefar part 2

Satans' Devices (tactics)

Before taking a look at his tactics, let's do a brief review of
part one:

First of all, we need to become aware that we are in a war.
Specifically, we are under attack from the evil ones, while
God is at work to grow us up spiritually. This is the war. We
are all the targets in this war: specifically, our minds are being
targeted to influence how we think because, as one Proverb
tells us, how we think determines how we <u>ARE</u>. This is the
true center of this warfare: God, working to bring His children
to maturity in life, and satan and his horde of evil beings
basically trying to kill us by influencing our thoughts.

At this point I think it needs to be said that all of this is
overseen by God: that is, as with Job, satan is only allowed to
do whatever God allows him to do. This is a very important
truth that I think few of us grasp and/or understand. Perhaps
we can explore this a bit more in a future writing. This is one
of satans' tactics: to try to get us to believe that he has sneaked
one over on God; that God has abandoned us in our present
situation, and that we are left to fight him on our own: this is a
gross lie! More on this later, but for now, let's acknowledge that
we are being attacked.

Next, that this is a SPIRITUAL war: that is, it must be

fought in the spirit realm. It is <u>NOT</u> a battle against people: this is another favored tactic of the enemy, to get us to focus on the people, but when we try to approach it that way, it is doomed, not only to fail, but also to do a LOT of damage.

Third, as brother Bob shared,

> *"<u>Jesus</u> came to destroy ("bring to naught") (the <u>Amplified version </u>adds this: undo; destroy; loosen and dissolve)the works of the Devil the works the devil [has done](<u>I Jn. 3:8</u>). How He does this is seen in the accounts of <u>Chapters 4 of Matthew and Luke</u>. As the admonition (above) makes clear, we are tempted to think that we first must feel an infusion of power or authority and then act on that power. Jesus did not do this. He first was led by the Spirit of God into the wilderness to fast. Jesus was in a weakened condition when Satan spoke to Him. Jesus' resisting of the Devil took the form of refusing to act apart from His Father.*
>
> *Satan's deception played on an acknowledgement that Jesus is the Son of God in order to coax Him into acting independent of the Father, relying instead on His position as Son of God. Jesus responded each time out of the reality that He is indeed the Son of God and <u>does not act independent of the Father</u>."*

<u>This is the primary focus of all the enemys' attacks: to get us to think or say or do something independent of the Father.</u>

He accomplishes this when he succeeds in persuading us to <u>THINK</u> apart from Father, because he knows that he will have drawn us away from Father, bringing death. (as with Eve, and Adam.)

Let's keep these first two firmly in mind, as we try to make a list of some of satans' devices, OK? Always remembering that satan is limited to whatever God allows, and always remembering that satan wants to influence us to get us as far away from God as he can: some tactics follow:

Of course there are always some well-known temptations that most of us know about: temptations, say, to lie, or cheat, or steal, or have sex with someone that's not ours, or rape somebody, or punch him in the face or kick him while he's down, or go to bad movies or look at porn or dirty dancing or drinking or smoking or chewing, etc. That list is almost unending, isn't it? But there are many more ways he uses to separate us from God: too many to list, really, but some follow that we might not typically see.

One very favorite one of his is to convince us that God didn't really mean what He said. This one has many facets, such as that it's obviously out-dated and can't possibly work in todays' world, or it's just not practical, or that God just wants to control you, etc.

Another one is that we don't really need God, because He has already given us the ability to think and analyze and decide stuff, so just use what he gave you: no need to be consulting Him about things: if you have a watch, there's no need to be asking anyone else what time it is; etc.

Yet another tactic is to get us very busy (with things that are "good", ya know: anything to get us so busy that we don't have time to spend talking with God or time to just be quiet with God and let Him talk to us.

Then there's "how you LOOK is very important, ya know, so spend as much time as possible making yourself look handsome or beautiful, and buy the best perfume or cologne, and just the right shade of lipstick, and have your hair done just so", etc.

Related to that one, is that you need to present yourself a certain approved way: never mind about how you actually ARE, it's how you APPEAR to others that matters. It's your IMAGE that counts, etc.

Of course there's always "it's YOU that really matters: ya gotta take care of #1." That's your FIRST concern, ya know. Sure, helping others is nice, but NEVER if it inconveniences YOU in any way . . .

And how about negativity? You should expect things not to turn out good; wait for the next shoe to fall; bad things happen in threes, ya know, and so far you've only had one or two . . . and related to this, there's dread, which is a fear about some unknown bad thing that may happen at any time in the future.

Worry: if something COULD go bad, it probably WILL, and the only thing to do is worry about it. In fact, if you DON'T worry, you probably don't even love yourself or that other person who might experience a bad thing. Worrying is a sure sign that you really CARE, etc.

Of course there's always "If it FEELS good, DO it": it's how you FEEL that's important! If someone else gets hurt, that's too bad, but NOT as important as how you feel.

A big one is "never trust God, or, for that matter, any other person: only trust yourself. You know you're the only one who truly understands your situation (or ANY situation, really)".

Say what you think: THAT's what's important (sure, you can listen to what other people say; even be polite) but it's what YOU think that's the important thing.

Well, THIS list could go on almost forever, as I'm sure you know, and you could surely make your own list if you wanted.

For the purpose of this writing, it's important, I think, to recognize that satan has developed a huge number of ways and means, but that his main purpose is to deter and distract us: to pull us away from God, because God is our Life, and he doesn't want us alive: he wants us dead. He knows that if he can get us to think his way, believe his lies and deceptions, and act accordingly, he will have accomplished his goal.

. . . <u>BUT GOD</u> . . .

Spurtchial Worefar part 3

In parts 1 & 2 of this series, we took a look at the reality of the spiritual attacks to which both we and others are subject . . . and a brief look at some of the devils' tactics/devices . . . in this writing, I am hoping to bring into focus what the Lord has given us to enable us to not only stand against, but to defeat the enemy when he attacks us in our personal circle of Life.

"For though we walk in the flesh, we do NOT war after the flesh: for the weapons of our warfare are not carnal, but mighty through God to the pulling down of strongholds; casting down imaginations, and every high thing that exalts itself against the knowledge of God, and bringing into captivity every thought to the obedience of Christ." (II Corinthians 10:3-5, KJV) . . . and . . .

"Finally, my brethren, be strong IN THE LORD, and in the power of HIS might. Put on the whole armor OF GOD, that you may be able to stand against the wiles of the devil. For we wrestle NOT AGAINST FLESH AND BLOOD, BUT AGAINST PRINCIPALITIES, AGAINST POWERS, AGAINST THE RULERS OF THE DARKNESS OF THIS WORLD, AGAINST SPIRITUAL WICKEDNESS IN HIGH PLACES. Wherefore take unto you the whole armor of God, that you may be able to withstand in the evil day, and having done all, to stand. Stand therefore, having your loins girded with TRUTH, and having on the breastplate of RIGHTEOUSNESS; and your feet shod with the preparation of THE GOSPEL OF

PEACE; above all, taking THE SHIELD OF FAITH, which will enable you to quench all the fiery darts of the wicked. And take THE HELMET OF SALVATION, and THE SWORD OF THE SPIRIT which is THE (in the now) WORD OF GOD. PRAYING always with all PRAYER AND SUPPLICATION IN THE SPIRIT, and being alert and watchful with perseverance and supplication for all saints." (Ephesians 6: 10–18, KJV)

The first of these scriptures states the foundation for parts 1 & 2 of this writing series: that we <u>ARE</u> in a war; that it is against spirit creatures and <u>NOT</u> against humans; that our weapons are not sourced in humans, but IN GOD; that it is our THOUGHTS that are being targeted (imaginations; strongholds); and that it is KNOWING GOD that is being assaulted, the basic temptation being to persuade us to think and/or say and/or do stuff independent of God.

Of course the first part of the second of these scriptures speaks of the same things. The second part speaks of how God has equipped us for these battles: how we are to depend on those things which God HAS already given us as we engage in this warfare. Most of us are familiar with the listing of "the whole armor of God" so my plan is to touch on these, lightly and then to proceed, in this writing, to a few other related thoughts.

So let's start with the thought that we need the <u>WHOLE</u> armor. Each "piece" of the armor has its own purpose, and because of the multi-faceted nature of the attacks of the enemy, we need (and have been given) ALL of the armor. Then let's not ever forget that this armor is <u>OF GOD</u>: that is, we are not supposed to be able to generate any of it ourselves. It is NOT (neither CAN it be) our human design or plan: it is <u>OF GOD</u>.

I have heard it taught that first thing in the morning, when you wake up, "ya gotta put yer armor on". (I was never quite sure just how you were supposed to DO that) . . . my question to some who have told me this is, "why did you take it off?" Our instruction from this scripture is to "take it unto yourself": not a single mention of taking it off for sleeping (or for any other reason). Now on to look at some of the specifics:

The girdle (belt) of TRUTH: this is absolutely needed; and a very BASIC need . . . truth . . . Remember: the enemys' basic tactic is lies and deception. Well (of course) the ONLY way to defeat those lies is TRUTH! I am told that brother <u>Paul</u> used this picture of a Roman soldiers' battle garb to illustrate for us how each piece of the armor is vital, and the "girdle" (or belt) is the basic piece of armor on which the other pieces depend: the breastplate, for example, is anchored on this belt; the scabbard for the sword is also attached to this belt, so it is extremely essential (the "belt" for the Roman soldier, and TRUTH for us) I do not think this can be over-stated. Jesus told us that Holy Spirit (in us) would lead us into "ALL TRUTH". Can we understand how important it is for us to know and to depend on the reality that "TRUTH", which is our foundational weapon, is "of God"? It (TRUTH) is brought to us BY HOLY SPIRIT, and apart from truth, no other armor is of any use. I think it is important also to keep in mind that Holy Spirit "brings this truth to us" when we are <u>IN</u> our battles.

RIGHTEOUSNESS: we have been made righteous by Jesus' sacrifice, and by the imparting to us of His very Life, which is our ONLY righteousness. (which all of us who are believing on Him DO have). Many attacks of the evil ones are against this reality, and our ONLY hope is to stand in agreement with the TRUTH of what God has done for us.

The GOSPEL OF PEACE "on our feet": that is, it is the TRUTH that God has reconciled us to Himself (made peace with us). THIS TRUTH is what enables us to walk into our battle without any fear! God is never "against us" (which is an idea that the evil ones would like us to be <u>LIE</u> ve). Once again, this "gospel of peace" is "OF (from) God".

The SHIELD OF FAITH . . . (which we are to "take") . . . Faith has its foundation in whatever God has said. God causes us to HEAR Him, which, when we believe, is FAITH. Apart from God saying a thing, there is no such thing as "faith", but when God HAS "said" something, THAT IS TRUTH, which when believed will refuse to accept or believe any other thing which the evil horde may throw our way.

The HELMET OF SALVATION, which speaks, I believe, of the guarding of our minds (our thoughts). SALVATION: our reality: not only our "escape from the fires of hell" (which of course it is) but also the reality of the giving to us of His Life, which is HOW we are saved. This reality (this TRUTH) is essential to keeping our thoughts in line with God.

The SWORD OF THE SPIRIT is the Word of God by which we Live. (Which scripture tells us, and which Jesus reiterated when He was tempted by the devil.) The Word (this is the "rhema" Word: that is, the Word which God is right now speaking: NOT the generally recorded and known "word", or even the scriptures, though of course He may very well be speaking to us THROUGH a scripture) This is, I believe, a very important distinction, and is at the heart of one of the primary ways the evil ones attack: they want us to believe that God has already said all He ever will say, because He has given us the scripture (our BIBLE). ONE problem with this is that very subtly it gets us depending on OUR OWN UNDERSTANDING of the scripture, and God has instructed us (in the scripture) NOT to depend on OUR OWN understanding: to say it ever-so-gently but straight out, <u>IT IS OUR UNDERSTANDING THAT HAS GOTTEN US INTO WHATEVER TROUBLE</u>

<u>WE PRESENTLY FIND OURSELVES</u>! But God has not changed, and He never will change, and throughout all of history, He has spoken to us humans. He is NOW (in our days) STILL "speaking" to us, and it is by THAT Word of His that we now Live.

PRAYER: this is the weapon that makes a direct contact between God and us. (and whoever it is for whom we are praying) It is greatly effective both for us individually and for everyone the Lord will bring to our attention; it is how we convey to Him our concerns and wants and felt needs; it is how we hold another before Him for Him to act on their behalf. Prayer is designed to be a two-way communication, so listening as we pray is mighty important! Hannah Hurnard sees prayer as how we channel Gods' wishes to another: it is like an umbilical cord between us and God, where our wants and needs are carried to Him and His responses are brought to us.

<u>James 4:7, KJV</u> gives us the basic instruction for spiritual warfare: "<u>*Submit yourselves therefore to God. Resist the devil, and he will flee from you*</u>". Submitting ourselves to God is receiving, believing, and acting upon TRUTH, Only God <u>IS</u> truth, and therefore it is only HE Who can and will guard and deliver us from the lies and deceptions that we have experienced and from which we continue to be tempted and attacked. Submitting ourselves to God must ALWAYS come BEFORE trying to do anything against the devil: not being submitted to God leaves us pitted against a vastly superior spiritual being, against whom we are NOT EQUIPPED. Of course we can only submit to God after we have HEARD Him (Faith), so as I see it, the FIRST thing we need to be about is getting ourselves submitted to Him in our present situations.

OK, so . . . a few other thoughts . . . weapons against the

evil ones: (keeping in mind always that these are given to us by God, and it is by His Life [His Power] that they are effective:

Obedience: we can always do stuff that we already know is given to us to be doing (doing good). This is true because, first of all, God has said it, and second of all, since He has said it, then it is His power that will accomplish it in us.

Taking our thoughts captive (related to obedience, but in our thought realm): we all decide how and what we think, and we have been given "the mind of Christ" to enable us to think His thoughts (and we have been given the instructions to think on *"whatever things are just, pure, lovely, of good report, virtuous, and praiseworthy", from Philippians 4:8, KJV*. This, of course, like all the other instructions, can only be done by Holy Spirit (but it CAN be done, since we HAVE Him inside us)

Refuse to Worry, and instead, TRUST. This is a great weapon because it "brings God" directly into all the situations we cannot "figger out". (which is a LOT, since wherever we now are, we are about to enter something we have never experienced before, therefore trusting the Lord is our only sane option)

Forgive everyone for everything: this one is huge for many of us, because we tend (unfortunately) the other way. Yet because *"It is God Who works in you, BOTH to WILL, AND TO DO His good pleasure"*: because of that, we CAN.

Be thankful . . . in, and FOR . . . everything! Challenging, of course, but (because of Him), doable!

I think it is good for us to begin to understand that these weapons are all aspects of THE LIFE which He has given us! We who believe HAVE ETERNAL LIFE! Which IS Gods' Life! Fight on, warriors!

First Things (In Tough Times)

What are ya supposed to do when tough times come? They do, ya know (come). I suppose most of us have heard that "<u>when tough times come, the tough get going</u>", or some such advice, and in "the church" many tell us we're supposed to just "<u>Praise the Lord</u>". Well I'm thinking there may be a good deal of truth to that, especially the latter, where we praise the LORD, and there is a very real foundational truth there, as I'm hoping we will catch a glimpse of by the time this writing is completed. (perhaps sometime this year) Here are a few Scriptures to think on next, about tough times:

1. - <u>John 16:33b, KJV</u> . . . (Jesus speaking) "<u>*in the world ye shall have tribulation: but be of good cheer; I have overcome the world*</u>".

2. - <u>Acts 14:22b, KJV</u> . . . (Paul & Barnabas talking to the church) "<u>*we must, through much tribulation, enter into the Kingdom of God*</u>".

3. - <u>I Thessalonians 5:18, KJV</u> . . ."<u>*In everything give thanks, for this is the will of God in Christ Jesus concerning you*</u>".

4. - <u>Romans 5:3b – 5, KJV</u> . . . "<u>*we glory in tribulations also; knowing that tribulation worketh patience; and patience, experience; and experience, hope: and hope maketh not ashamed; because the Love of God is shed abroad in our hearts by the Holy Ghost which is given unto us*</u>".

5. - James 1: 2b – 4, KJV . . . *"count it all joy, when you fall in to divers temptations; knowing this, that the trying of your faith worketh patience. But let patience have her perfect work, that ye may be perfect and entire, wanting nothing".*
6. - Hebrews 10:36, KJV . . . *"For ye have need of patience, that after ye have done the will of God, ye might receive the promise".*
7. - James 5: 7&8, KJV . . . *"Be patient therefore, brethren, unto the coming of the Lord. Behold, the husbandman waiteth for the precious fruit of the earth, and hath long patience for it, until he receive the early and latter rain. Be ye also patient; establish your hearts; for the coming of the Lord draweth nigh".*
8. - Luke 21:19, KJV . . . (Jesus speaking) *"In your patience possess ye your souls".*

These scriptures (among other things) teach us about first things from Gods' perspective, which I believe is where we all desire to get. In our human experience, however, we tend NOT to be there (at least not at first). When something hurts, it HURTS, fer goodness sake, and there is no way to avoid feeling that pain, no matter how many people give us their "good advice". I for one do not think there is any problem when we express that pain: crying; anger; fist-shaking, etc. The prollem is that we tend to get stuck there. We tend not to "rise above it", so to speak, but these scriptures speak to us of a different, BETTER way: so how do we GET there? How do we get "above ground"?; into the positive, from our negative? I hope in the rest of this writing to point us "upward".

I'm thinking the path to that involves wrestling with some of the following: basically, wrestling with what we actually believe in our hearts about God.

Since I was a young guy (yup, I really WAS young once) growing up in the church, I heard four basic things about God:

First, that God is "omni-present", which means that He is everywhere: and also means that there ain't nowhere that He ain't! Now THAT's something to think about don't ya think? . . . Everywhere . . . I'm thinking that means He is RIGHT HERE in the middle of my mess; my pain; my ache: right <u>HERE</u>! I suppose if any of us really thought about that, we would be forced to agree, So He's HERE.

So what? . . . Well . . .

The next thing I was taught about this is that He is "Omniscient", which means that He knows . . . EVERYTHING! . . . Or to say it another way, there ain't nothing He don't know! Ya mean He knows everything there is to know about my stuff?, specifically that He knows EVERY detail of what I'm going through right now? . . . yup . . . that's what He tells us. So He's here in the middle of my situation, and He knows every cotton-pickin' thing about it? I suppose I can believe that too, but again, so what?

Well the third thing I heard is that He is "omnipotent", which means that He don't have any limits on what He can do. He can do ANYTHING! (And of course, that there ain't nothing He CAN'T do) So He could FIX this situation if He wanted to? Once again the answer is "yup, He COULD". Well if THAT's true, then why in heck don't He fix it? Well, this leads us directly to the next point. (and possibly one other one after that)

That point is that as I also heard, He is LOVE! And I'm thinking that THIS one is the hardest to understand of all the points so far: Love . . . Don't we all have in our heads some idea of what "Love" is supposed to look like? Don't we? And the thing we tend to be thinking about this (when we're in the middle of our suffering and pain), is (I'm pretty sure) "if He really loved me, and if He really IS here in my trial, and if He really KNOWS ALL ABOUT IT, and if He really COULD do something about it, but DOESN'T, then HOW in the world could THIS be love? A very good question, I'm thinking, and what we have to wrestle with NOW is the idea that HIS idea of Love must be a lot different from MY idea of it . . . and THAT is precisely where our problem arises, and because of how we've been brought up to believe (about Love), it is perfectly natural for us to think that way . . . BUT . . .

I'm talking here in this writing to those who WANT things to be Gods' way: who have begun to understand that HIS way and OUR ways are NOT THE SAME. Here's the thing: The Love which God IS is not occupied only with present moment things. He is an eternal Being, and He thinks eternal thoughts: that is, as the scriptures quoted above tell us, there is PURPOSE in our trials, and it is not His primary purpose to relieve us of our pain (of whatever sort): not His PRIMARY purpose. (Though He intimately knows our pain and struggles, etc., as we have seen above) Rather, He is PRIMARILY about accomplishing in us and for us a thing which HE knows, and WE do NOT. This is the main distinguishing element of His Love (the Love which HE IS): He is always out to bring us to the highest, greatest, best for us, which necessarily (for us) means that we gotta sometimes go through very great difficulties. And this leads us to what I think is the last point for this writing:

That is, that God is . . . well . . . God is GOD! Which means, ya know, that HE made everything there is; that He is managing and directing and controlling and energizing and maintaining everything there IS, and that HE will bring all of

His purposes to fulfillment. That is <u>HIS</u> "part": And (alas, dear heart), you and I do not (and <u>CAN</u>not) do any of that . . . WE belong to HIM, and it is HIS "job" to take care of us, and HE claims that HE will do it! Can ya believe it?

So . . . while we are considering our own tough times, maybe it would help us to consider these points? Maybe starting with this last one, and then going backwards through the list? Maybe? So if we're in pain, I think it's OK to cry or to yell or to shake our fist at heaven: however we initially respond, but it seems to me that it is far best for us to get to the place where these points (above) become solidly set in the foundation of our being. Rebuking the devil is, I've heard, a popular and accepted, typical response to our trials: but if God is what we've written above, that makes no sense, and will not be effective. If God is Who we've said, (and I ain't taking it back) then the devil cannot have any access to us unless God has specifically permitted him; and if God has permitted him, then God will continue to use that evil one until he has completed Gods' purpose. (Which is our good) In such a case, when we think we are "rebuking the devil" we are in fact actually rebuking God (and that just ain't gonna work), cuz HE IS GOD, ya know, (and we are not). Well, you get the picture.

In some of her Writings, Hannah Hurnard uses the phrase, ACCEPTANCE WITH JOY to describe a healthy response for us when facing difficult events in our lives; when things are not going like we think they should. It is the only good, healthy response in those times after we have gotten through our initial responses. THEN, we can begin our dialog with God, and He will show us how to go through whatever we need to go through. He has promised us His strength (His Grace) for our trials: HE will bring us THROUGH our test! Let's do it GODS' way!

Now I AM aware that there are many who do not really WANT things to go Gods' way, cuz they aren't really willing for things NOT to go THEIR way, but that's not you . . . is it?

Christmas

Christmas . . . Christ-mas . . . Christ celebration: that's what the word means: Celebration of Christ! So I'm wondering: How many of us even know what THAT means?

For most of us, at least in this country, it means cutting or buying a small-ish evergreen tree; bringing it into our homes, putting it onto some sort of stand; "decorating" it with our choice of lights, balls, other ornaments, tinsel, icicles, etc. and topping it with a star, or maybe an "angel".

It also means making or (more likely) going to a bunch of stores to buy presents for our family and some friends, then bringing them home; wrapping them with festive paper and ribbons and bows, and putting them under the tree to wait until "Christmas" day.

Then a bunch of us gather to unwrap those gifts, hopefully expressing our thanks to whoever bought them and wrapped them for us; then gathering up all the remnants of paper and ribbons, trashing some and saving some for "next Christmas".

Of course, besides decorating our tree, we have also decorated a good portion of our home. We play nice "Christmas music, like "White Christmas", or "Rudolph the Red-nosed Reindeer", or "Here comes Santa Claus".

Then there is, of course, the great banquet over which we have toiled and planned for many days: there are many variations of this for different families, to be sure.

But I am wondering: WHERE (in all this) is CHRIST, whose birth we are supposedly celebrating? How many of us know WHO or WHAT Christ is? Many have put an X in the place of Christ, making it "X-mas" . . . celebrating "X"? Just having a celebration for the fun of it! Nothing necessarily bad about that, is there? After all, fun IS fun, isn't it? Party On!

But for those of us who want to celebrate Christ, let's think a bit: Are we wanting to have a birthday party for Jesus? Why? Is He just another birthday to be remembered, along with those of our family and friends? Or isn't it rather quite a bit MORE than that?

Celebration of Christ: it all began (for us humans) a bit over 2,000 years ago in the small middle-east village of Nazareth. There was a young man there whose name was Joseph. Joseph was a carpenter, and he was "espoused" (that's a bit like "engaged", but much more detailed, and serious), to a teen-aged girl named Mary.

Well, one day, while Mary was going about doing whatever little Jewish teen-agers do, suddenly, with no warning whatsoever, POOF! An Angel! Right in front of her! And he said to her, "Hail!" (Which I think is a lot like "HI" with a bunch of exclamation marks after it). "Hail, you who are highly favored! The Lord is with you! Out of all women, YOU are blessed!" Well, as I'm sure you can imagine, Mary was "troubled" and trying to figure out what in the world was going on.

But the angel told her not to be afraid (so she wasn't), and also that she was about to conceive and bear a son whom she should name "Jesus". Mary was puzzled and asked the angel how that could happen, since she had never been with any man that way. The angel then explained that the Holy Spirit would "come upon her" and that the power of the Highest would "overshadow" her, so her son would be called "The Son of God". He went on to tell her that with God, NOTHING would be impossible: and although I'm sure she did not really understand all this, she yielded herself and told the angel that she was willing for all this to happen, and she presented herself as "the handmaiden of the Lord".

After a few months it was getting clear to Joseph that Mary's tummy was growing and it was not long before He knew that his Mary was expecting, though he also knew the baby was not his. What was he to do? He didn't want her harmed, but he didn't feel he could marry her with another man's baby in her tummy so he finally decided to divorce her quietly and privately.

Before he could carry out his plan, however, one night, in a dream, an angel appeared to HIM, explaining things to him and told him not to be afraid to take Mary as his wife, so soon there was a wedding.

Shortly afterward, the government sent out a notice that everyone was to return to his birth-place to register and be taxed. Joseph was from Bethlehem, so he and Mary set out for Bethlehem (about a three-day trip).

Somewhere along the way (hopefully close to Bethlehem) the labor pains started, and Mary knew they would need to find some place for her baby to be born. They tried an inn, but the inn had no vacancies! There WAS a stable out behind the inn, however, and the inn-keeper said they were welcome to stay there, so they went into that stable and tried to get as comfortable as possible in the hay and straw that was there, along with the animals.

Before long the Baby came: THE Baby, Son of the Highest, God. Jesus, Who was to save His people from their sins: There He was, a new-born infant. Mary wrapped Him in some cloths and laid Him in the place where the animals ate. It seemed only Mary and Joseph (and the animals, of course) were there to witness His birth! I wonder what they were thinking and feeling?

BUT . . . as it turns out, they were NOT the only ones to witness His arrival: a HUGE bunch of heavenly creatures saw it and THEY celebrated! Christmas! How they celebrated!!! The very FIRST celebration of Christ! The first Christmas EVER!

It happened this way: it was night time, and in a nearby field there were some shepherds keeping their eyes on a bunch of sheep, and SUDDENLY, without any warning (just like with Mary) POOF! An Angel! A very bright angel appeared to them and the Glory of the Lord shone all around them . . . THEY were TERRIFIED!

But (just like with Mary) the angel told them not to be afraid, because he was there to bring them some very good news!: great, joyful news for everyone! Right now, he told them: right here in Bethlehem the Savior has been born: Christ, the Lord! He said they would know Him when they found a baby, wrapped in cloths and lying in a feeding trough.

And if THAT wasn't enough, SUDDENLY a huge crowd of heavenly beings appeared with the angel, praising God: Glory to God in the highest! Peace on earth! Good will to men!

And then they all disappeared back to heaven and the shepherds hot-footed it into town and found the baby (the Savior), just as the angel said: the baby in the manger and Mary and Joseph nearby.

After a while they left, telling whoever they met all about what had happened to them! Then back to their sheep, glorifying and praising God for it all!

OK . . . so that's how the FIRST Christmas was . . . Heavenly beings, an angel, and a bunch of lowly shepherds, all praising and glorifying God! The Son of God had come to earth as a baby: Our Savior!

And He DID become our Savior! As a pre-teen He conversed regularly with the religious leaders of that time, and they were astounded at His wisdom and knowledge. When He was about 30 He chose 12 men to follow and learn from Him, going about teaching them as well as crowds of others the things of God's Kingdom. He healed all kinds of diseases and even raised some from the dead. He told them (and us, too) that God's Love is such that He gave His Son to die in place of all of us so we would not die, but rather, we could have everlasting, eternal life: <u>IF</u> we will believe in Him.

This "believing" is a heart thing: not a head thing. It is total dependence only on Him to give us this Life.

When He was about 33 years old, the religious leaders who at first admired Him became jealous of Him; then fearful: then ragingly angry, to the point that they convinced the Roman authorities to crucify Him, which they did. To all His friends this was a horrible tragedy, but this death, which He willingly accepted in their place and in ours was actually a magnificent triumph over the power of sin! We no longer have to face that terror . . . IF we will only believe! . . . (in our hearts)

But the celebration does not stop there because in three days God raised Him out of death, and after several more days God took Him from the earth back into Heaven. For us who believe, He gives His Life (birth, death, resurrection, ascension) . . . <u>NOW!</u> THAT whole package is worthy of great celebration!

<u>Merry Christ-mas!</u>

Are you wondering if it's OK for you to have a tree and decorations and presents and feasting? Perhaps: I'm not sure: to me personally, those things tend to cloud over and distract me from truly celebrating Christ. I don't see anything wrong with those things in and of themselves (unless we are participating in an old pagan ritual from which many of these practices were taken): however, for me the question remains, regardless of how we celebrate, is Christ genuinely the object of our celebration?

Also, this celebration needs to be first of all something that is true in my heart. If that is not truly in my heart, then NO festivities will truly be a "Christ-mas"

What does a true "Christ-mas" look like? I am thinking it will probably look a lot like that of those Heavenly Beings . . . and those shepherds . . . Thanking and praising and glorifying God for bringing THAT baby into our world: THAT baby Who would become our Savior; our Lord; our leader; our teacher; and our Life!

<u>Have a truly wonderful "Christ-mas"!</u>

"You Got It!"

"With God all things are possible", He said: "Ask (and keep on asking) and it will be given you", He said: "If you, being evil (*what?: me? . . . evil?*) give good things to YOUR children, how much more will your Heavenly Father give what is good to those who ask?", He said: "Everyone who asks receives", He said: EVERYONE? . . . REALLY? . . . Well HE said it, not me.

Then He told a couple of stories to let us know that we should keep on asking (be persistent, ya know), and not give up: how long, I wonder? Then He asks a question at the end of one of those stories: "when the Son of Man comes (not "if" He comes: "when" He comes. Seems pretty clear that He intends to come . . . WHEN He comes), will He find faith on the earth? . . . Wha? What in the world does this mean, "find faith on the earth"? Seems like He's implying that we should be looking for Him to come (in answer to our prayer) until He actually comes with His answer, however long that takes?

Then He said a really WEIRD thing: "Everything (really? EVERYTHING?) you ask in prayer", He said, "believe you HAVE received them", He said, "and they (even more than one thing?) will be granted to you" Really? Well, that's what He said! (I can give you the references if you'd like)

But really: believe I HAVE received them? Wouldn't that be dishonest? Obviously I don't have them, or I wouldn't be asking for them, right? Is He asking me to try to trick my mind into believing I've got something I really DON'T got? Somehow that don't seem right! He must mean some other thing! but WHAT? What could He possibly mean?

So I'm talking at Him about this a few days ago, and THIS pops into my mind (or wherever those kind of things pop to): a couple of days ago I went to visit one of my favorite restaurants, and pretty soon after they led me to a table and gave me a menu, a waitress came by and asked me what I would like, so I told her what I would like, and guess what she said? "YOU GOT IT", she said! I got it? It wasn't on my table and she's telling me I got it? But I noticed that for some reason I didn't have a problem with her saying that! Amazing! Somehow (don't ask me how) I understood that when she said "You Got It", she was telling me (without saying any more words) that she would write my wishes on a piece of paper; that she would then take that piece of paper to some other people who would read her paper; and that because those people could understand what she had written and why she had written it: because of that and because of what their job was and because of their skills and resources (I could go on and on, but I think you got the point) Anyway, those people would create the stuff I wanted; let the waitress know when it was ready for her to bring to me; and very soon she would pick up my stuff from them and bring it to me. (their creation, her delivery), right to my very table! So NOW . . . "I Got It". But I'm thinking that because of the reputation of that restaurant with its resources, and the nature of its employees, when my waitress said, "You Got It", that I could count on the certainty of "getting It" right when I placed my order: even well before it appeared on my table ! I "believed that I had received it", and I got it!

So . . . "With God ALL things are possible" . . . He owns it ALL, they say, and He is unlimited in power, they say . . . and HE WANTS to give us good things, He said.

Well I didn't have any problem believing my waitress, but I am wondering: will I have any problems believing God?; that I am one of the "everyone" who receives what he asks?; who believes I have received it, when I ask?; who will be found in faith (expecting His answer) and waiting for Him to appear with it ?

Will I? . . . Will YOU?

I don't know the answer to either question . . . I'm just trying to tell us both what He said.

Printed in the United States
By Bookmasters